Urbanreviews.com
The cover of this book says it all: If you did not know this is a statue of King Tut, you NEED to read this book. *We Ain't No Niggas!* **shows the grave imbalance** in what has and has not been taught about African and African-American History. The author gives historical, documented facts on how Africa was the birthplace of civilization. There is **a wealth of information in this book** that's just simply priceless. ...[T]his book should be **required reading for all African-Americans.**

Greg D., Georgia
For this book to be published in the era of gangster novels is nothing short of a miracle. Brother Cincere has such a **passion for truth and justice** that his words literally jump off the pages! This book is packed with pictures that I have never seen in my life, and I have read tons of books. This is the type of information you just can't put a price on. I will go as far to say this is **the most informative book on African history since the dawning of this new millennium.**

O'OSA Online Book Club
Cincere's WE AIN'T NO NIGGAS! is designed to help you make sense of what is out there, or in many cases, not out there. It sheds light on **hidden and/or little known facts and truths**. In this book, you will find clear, easy-to-understand information... WE AIN'T NO NIGGAS! is the perfect start, providing **enlightening, positive and empowering knowledge.**

Cultural Educators of Toronto , Canada
'We Ain't No Niggas' is **a profound piece of work** that will tap your pineal gland...open up your chakras and implant the concepts that were taken away from you during slavery. This book is **a study guide and is a must have** for anyone claiming to be afrocentric, pan african or the likes...this book is a needed companion of any one who loves to learn...**learn from this book who you really are**, because We Ain't No Niggas!

Naturalmystic, New York
Balance is the key and this book **vividly and explicitly annotated the imbalance in our world history education**. I always knew that something was out of sync...This book puts it all in perspective and I am committed to learning more and sharing it with others. **It's about time, someone told the truth.**

Presented by:

Please visit:
www.knowledgeofselfpublishing.com

email:
info@knowledgeofselfpublishing.com

or write:
Knowledge of Self Publishing
P.O. Box 1010
California, Maryland 20619

Knowledge of Self Publishing, LLC
Permissions Department
P.O. Box 1010
California, Maryland 20619

www.knowledgeofselfpublishing.com

ISBN-10:   0-9787862-0-3
ISBN-13: 978-0-9787862-0-5

Registered with United States Library of Congress. Includes content notes, bibliographical references and index.

Original artwork of King Cetewayo on page 115 by freelance artist Mr. Phice Richardson (mrprichda@comcast.net). Cover design by Daryl T. Hinmon.

We Ain't No Niggas!
Exposing the Deception of YOUR World History Education
N. Quamere Cincere
Foreword by Daryl T. Hinmon

WARNING - DISCLAIMER

This book is intended to provide not very well publicized historical facts as documented by past and present historians, intellectuals, professors, etc. Both the author and publisher have gone through great lengths to ensure the accuracy of this text, but there is a chance some human errors may exist. The reader is strongly encouraged to read other texts that both agree with and oppose documented facts presented here to get the full picture of History. This book is not offered as an all encompassing history book, but rather as a guideline to offer the reader a different perspective of the History discipline. The author and the publisher assume no responsibility and neither shall have any responsibility greater than the price of this book for any direct or indirect damage believed to have been caused by any information contained herein this book. Please feel free to contact the publisher for a full refund of the purchase price if you do not agree to be bound by the above disclaimer, otherwise your purchase constitutes agreement.

Acknowledgements and Dedication:

Thanks to the Creator for my faith, my health, my family and my familys' faith, health, peace and serenity. Thanks to all the Master Teachers, Speakers and Preachers throughout eternity, I am your sponge. Thanks to my tribe The Hinmons, The Palmers, The Downings, The Arringtons and The Johnsons. Thanks to Mr. Bodsworth, Mrs. D. Thompson, The Shearns, Mr. & Mrs. Miller, Mr. Parker and Ms. Desper.

Much love and respect to the City of Philadelphia for my hunger and inspiration - especially Bernard Hopkins and Jill Scott. Thanks to Mr. Reckley, Mr. Fleetwood, Mr. Blank, Mrs. Hamilton, Mrs. Levinson, Mr. Hubbard, Mr. Gainey, Brother P.A., K.T., Ms. V. Brown, Ma. P, Mrs. Williams, Mrs. Y., Raq and Mr. Norman.

Peace and love to my Mother and Father, true soldiers! Thank you to every Aunt and every Uncle for your example. To The Wife, I love you infinitely. Much love to DaShaunta, Darian, Tyrone, Darrenae, Darlesheia, Nasier, Savoy, Dantaeyah, Rasheem, Sean, Shopel, Shaquan, Sommer, Malachi, Quarmere, Noah a.k.a. Big Willie, Darren, Marvin, Victor, Stacy, Nadiyah and O.Y.-T.I.F.Y. Chenelle. I'm watching you to both teach and to learn. Welcome to the world Dajah Renee!

Dr. V. Cowell, you influenced me more than you'll ever know. Peace to the greatest mentor in the world: William Campbell. Peace to the real Brothers strengthening our existence: Delwyn, Raynon, Damon, Willie, Tracy, Keith, Jay, Walt, Yuron and my Brother Daryl Carter. R.I.P.: Shawanda Townsend, Dr. Howard Alford, Mr. 'K.C.' Fennell and Uncle Jack...I miss you man.

This book is dedicated to all those who came before me and those who will follow. My strength is your strength. Black people of the world: chins up, shoulders back and chests out when you read this!

Table of Contents

Table of Figures

Foreword

Christopher Columbus was the first European to stumble upon the "New World". The reason Europeans referred to the Americas as the "New World" is because it was new to them. The fact of the matter is ancient Africans voyaged to what is now known as North, South and Central Americas and the West Indian islands hundreds of years before Columbus was a twinkle in his daddy's eyes. It is documented that Mansa Musa, King of the Mali Empire in Western Africa, and many other ancient Africans sent voyagers across the Atlantic to trade with indigenous inhabitants of the Americas years before Columbus' outings. Professor Ivan Van Sertima documented this fact in *They Came Before Columbus.* Dr. Ishakamusa Barashango and Professor John G. Jackson also provided scholarly pieces documenting pre-Columbus African voyages. In fact, Africans had been sailing thousands of years before Columbus' existence as evidenced by Pharaoh Khufu's Solar Barge dated back to 2600 B.C., therefore, it only makes sense they would reach the "New World" before Europeans. (Khufu's Solar Barge is pictured and discussed by Mr. Cincere in the chapter titled *What You Were Not Taught.)* Some of these pre-Columbus African

Foreword

voyagers had such positive relations in the New World that they decided to settle here. Africans' settlement of these lands is convincingly evidenced by ancient African artifacts found in the Americas (the Olmec heads for example). Additionally, colonies of black people were observed in Mexico, Central America, South America and the West Indian islands by the visiting Europeans some years later. Things were good for Africans in the Americas during those times.

After European imperialism in Africa and the arrival of the first Europeans in the Americas in the late 1400's, things began to get rough for Africans. Imperialist Europeans in Africa and America introduced the concept of African inferiority. Based on their fallible conclusion that Africans were inferior to Europeans, they enslaved, physically abused, mentally conditioned, spiritually raped, conceptually dehumanized and utterly disrespected Africans already in the Americas and those brought here against their will under trans-Atlantic slavery. European Americans figuratively and sometimes literally branded a sub-human label upon Africans worldwide, particularly those in America. In fact, it took almost three hundred years for the 'Founding Fathers' to finally recognize Africans in America as $3/5^{ths}$ of a person in the Constitution. But even this unsteady recognition was only on paper -- and in all honesty only for political reasons -- for in reality African Americans living in the southern states post-Constitution were still enslaved, burdened with their imposed sub-human status and treated as $0/5^{ths}$ of a human. After another hundred years of degradation, humiliation, mutilation and exploitation, the Emancipation Proclamation (1863) and 13th Amendment of the Constitution (1865) finally declared African Americans full $5/5^{ths}$ human beings. Again this declaration was only on paper and not in practice, for in reality, African Americans were still openly oppressed, freely lynched, socially segregated and treated as only part-human well into the 1960's. Even to this day, African Americans are at best treated

Foreword

as 4/5ths human i.e. second class citizens as evidenced most recently by the Hurricane Katrina fiasco in New Orleans.

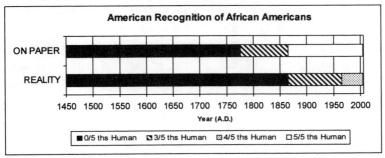

During the first few hundred years of our great nation's existence, the foundation of the American way of life was developed by a biased society who largely considered African Americans (Negroes) UN-HUMAN! As verified in this 1863 Harper's Weekly picture, African Americans were thought to be no more than animals.

CUTTING HIS OLD ASSOCIATES.
MAN OF COLOR. "Ugh! Get out. I ain't one ob you no more. I'se a Man, I is!"

White Americans thought Negroes were ugly, ignorant and ultimately inferior to themselves; they openly spoke it and boldly wrote it. Unfortunately, these same European Americans, who according to today's social standard were 'racists', formed the basis of America's legal, political, social, financial and most

Foreword

importantly educational structures. These mentally skewed early Americans developed the American Education system with the equations European=superior, African=inferior foremost in their minds. During this time period, the what, where, why and how young Americans would be taught was determined by self-proclaimed 'superior' European Americans! The same European Americans who strongly believed in the superiority of their own race/culture and the inferiority of the African race/culture laid the foundation of what, where, why and how all young Americans would be taught about the history of the world, including all the people of the world. The same genre of European Americans who determined that blacks only equated to $0/5^{ths}$, $3/5^{ths}$ or some other fraction of a person, influenced the basis of how and exactly what all current and future Americans would be taught about their history.

Well respected Harvard and Yale educated scholars such as Dr. Jeffries Wyman and Dr. Thomas Savage who in 1847 asserted that the closest link between man and beast is represented by the Negro and orangutan influenced what all Americans would be taught about Africans and African Americans.[1] In 1900 another scholar named Dr. Paul B. Barringer wrote about hereditary savagery in Negro blood, how slavery was able to manage the inherent savagery, and ultimately how the Negro would return to his savage state without the institution of slavery. He also influenced American education.[2] Dr. Barringer's broad sphere of influence goes without saying as he was the sixth President of Virginia Tech, headed the Medical Preparatory School at Davidsonville College, and served as Chair of Physiology and Chairman of Faculty at the University of Virginia. Harvard educated Professor Nathaniel Southgate Shaler, who became a dean at Harvard, wrote about the savage nature of Negroes in the late 1800's.[3] Dr. William Shockley was educated at M.I.T., taught at Stanford and made repeated public references to the inferiority of black people well

Foreword

into the 20th century. Dr. Robert Bennett Bean, who was educated at Johns Hopkins, somehow came to a medical conclusion in the early 1900's that the brains of white people were more advanced and superior to the brains of blacks. Dr. Bean's influence was direct as he undoubtedly taught this culturally biased theory to his students at the University of Michigan, Tulane University and the University of Virginia.[4] Professor James Henry Breasted was known as the 'Father of American Egyptology' and taught at the University of Chicago. He made frequent references to the "Great White Race" in his mid-1900's books that were used as text books in American History classes.[5] One of his books, *Ancient Times: A History of the Early World*, has numerous references to the "Great White Race" and was used as a text book in a Maryland high school. A check-out card from a Maryland high school library copy of *Ancient Times* is on the following page. This book most likely was used in many other high schools across the nation as Professor Breasted was a well respected, world renowned historian.

Powerful men who agreed with the concept of white superiority and black inferiority influenced the educational discipline of history in our country. Even past American political leaders - George Washington, Abraham Lincoln, Thomas Jefferson, Theodore Roosevelt, William Howard Taft, Benjamin Tillman, Eugene Talmadge and the infamous George Wallace - openly expressed their feelings of 'negro inferiority' and negatively influenced what all current and future Americans would be taught about Africans and African Americans. And this only represents a short list of those American leaders who voiced their opinion, not even considering those who shared those feelings, but only expressed them during political votes.[6]

Foreword

DATE DUE	BORROWER'S NAME	ROOM NUMBER
	901	8154
	Breasted, James Henry	
	AUTHOR	
	Ancient Times: A History of the	
	TITLE	
	Early World	
SEP 22 '66	Cheryl	10
OCT 4 '66	James	Mrs Gee 35
OCT 18 '66		
NOV 2 '66	John	
	Mrs	96
NOV 17 '66		Pennington
NOV 27 '66		
DEC 15 '66	Agnes	34 Sutton
JAN 18 '67	Delois	H-J
FEB 1 '67	Lois	Evans
FEB 2	Betty	Mrs. Race
29 '67	Mike	

*All the students (black or white) who used this book during Miss Sutton, Miss Pennington's, Miss Ellen's, Mrs. Gee's and Mrs. Evans' classes learned the "Great White Race" developed civilization while black Africans had nothing to do with it.

Many early American historians depicted people of African descent as inferior, ignorant and savage in their history

Foreword

books. The very same history books used to teach generations of Americans! History as taught in our country was and to a lesser extent still is biased because the people who laid the foundation of history were biased. A biased historian cannot write an unbiased history. Subsequently, a history that stands on a biased foundation cannot stand erectly in an unbiased manner. Its footing is skewed, therefore, the body must be skewed as well. Due to these circumstances, true and full history was never introduced into the American education system. One may suppose sometime after African Americans were finally recognized as whole people there was some futile attempt to remove the bias, but obviously it did not happen to the extent necessary for African Americans to regain their depth and dignity after hundreds of years of sustained oppression. As a consequence, some African Americans persecute themselves because they do not know who they are. A demography of African Americans consistently demean, disrespect, put down, disgrace, maim and even murder themselves, many times with neither hesitation nor moral consequence because they did not receive a proper Knowledge of Self in their standard education. African Americans were subliminally instructed not to respect themselves and not to expect respect from others. They were taught that they were slaves here in America:

> ➢ whipped into submission
> ➢ shackled in chains
> ➢ constantly disrespected sub-human citizens

They were taught that they were ignorant savages in Africa:

> ➢ uncivilized in African jungles
> ➢ sub-human voodoo cannibals
> ➢ running around naked, yipping and yelping

And they were taught these concepts from history books written predominantly by European Americans from the then biased European American perspective. They know the negative facets of their history, but many are largely unfamiliar with the positive.

Foreword

They are unfamiliar with the true and full history of themselves; therefore they do not command a proper Knowledge of Self necessary to improve their collective mental state and develop the confidence necessary to take action towards closing political, social and financial performance gaps that exist in our country today.

Knowledge of Self Publishing, L.L.C. **is dedicated** to publishing books that are dedicated to balancing history. *We Ain't No Niggas! Exposing the Deception of YOUR World History Education* by Mr. Nasier Quamere Cincere does just that. Knowledge of Self Publishing is proud to present you our flagship publication, for your reading and learning pleasure. N. Quamere Cincere has composed an easy to read, in your face, intellectual masterpiece that really does expose the deception in your World History education. This book **IS REQUIRED READING FOR EVERY AFRICAN AMERICAN** and beneficial reading for all European Americans. As he states, "Each letter of each word counts as a weight in helping to balance your education." His logic will resound in your heart and the hard core documentation and pictures will open your eyes to the TRUTH! After Mr. Cincere lays the ground rules in the beginning of the book, he gets physical in bringing his point home throughout the rest of the text (especially the chapter *What You Were Not Taught*). In fact, we at Knowledge of Self Publishing feel so certain that you will learn something new about World History and/or get the opportunity to see World History from a different perspective that we GUARANTEE it. It is unprecedented in the publishing industry to offer a MONEY BACK GUARANTEE on a book, but this is an unprecedented book. Therefore, here is our:

Foreword

> # MONEY BACK GUARANTEE!
> If after reading this text in its entirety you have not learned anything new and have not experienced a different perspective of History, contact the publisher for a full refund of the purchase price! *

*Only the ultimate consumer (reader) is eligible for the Money Back Guarantee. Contact Knowledge of Self Publishing for details.

I know the excitement you will feel as you read this text, so feel free to email either Mr. Cincere or myself as we share the same excitement. Enjoy!

Respectfully Submitted,
Daryl T. Hinmon, Publisher
dth@knowledgeofselfpublishing.com

Part A: *Introduction*

The Negro... has obstacles, discouragements, and temptations to battle with that are little known to those not situated as he is. When a white... undertakes a task, it is taken for granted that he will succeed. On the other hand, people are usually surprised if the Negro... does not fail. In a word, the Negro... starts out with a presumption against him.

The influence of ancestry, however, is important in helping forward any individual or race.[1]

**Booker T. Washington
1900**

1. *Knowledge of Self*

Over 100 years ago, Mr. Booker T. Washington recognized the critical role knowledge of self plays in the upliftment of any one person or race of people. On page 36 of his autobiography *Up From Slavery*, Mr. Washington explicitly states "[t]he influence of ancestry . . . is important in helping forward any individual or race."[1] European Americans can fully appreciate Mr. Washington's statement as they have realized the influence of their ancestry, which has played an important role in forwarding their culture or race. In fact, the ancestry of the European American as presented in any American classroom has reaped an intoxicating benefit of empowerment to the European American as the negative aspects of their history have been filtered out and the positive aspects exaggerated. The current stupendous financial, social and political positions of European Americans are a direct result of them receiving a very biased knowledge of themselves through the education system. The benefit of the Europeans' knowledge of himself is magnified as their education persistently glorifies their past conquests and accomplishments while nonchalantly concealing major

3

embarrassments, especially the time in history when Europeans were dominated by others.

On the other hand, or on the other side of the tracks, there is the African American. African Americans have been operating with a severe handicap as they have been trying to forward their race for hundreds of years without full knowledge of their ancestry. It is impossible for any African American who depends solely on the education system for knowledge of themselves to realize the positive influence of their ancestry in forwarding their culture or race. Unlike their European counterparts, African Americans do not have the luxury of a curriculum that consistently highlights their momentous historical accomplishments while tactfully concealing the historical low-points of their culture. In fact African Americans have the exact opposite, a curriculum that specifically concentrates on every low period in the history of African Americans and people of African descent and tactfully ignores their numerous majestic historical periods.[2] Unlike European Americans, African Americans have not realized the psychological benefit of the persistent glorification of their culture through the American education curriculum. The aggregate positive aspects of African history are barely mentioned, nevertheless glorified. Some positive achievements of individual Africans and African Americans may have been mentioned during Black History month, but the glorification of African culture as a whole is absent. In fact, the history of people of African descent seems reversed filtered from that of the European. Most of the positive African historical accomplishments, particularly the time in history they have dominated other cultures, have been eliminated from or was never included in the curriculum. At the same time, the low periods in the history of people of African descent are aggressively promoted in school. This lethal combination of historical manipulation severely hampers the African Americans' ability to forward their culture. The message sent to society

4

about African and African American ancestry through the modern day education is most blacks are niggas and a nigga never amounted to anything, nor are they expected to amount to anything. Despite being manipulated by today's education and consequently missing the influence of their full ancestry, African Americans have made decent financial, social and political strides over the last 400 years. Now the time to reach their full operating position has come.

In order to even the proverbial playing field, both European Americans and African Americans need to be taught the true and full history of all people. All sides of all stories must be equally stressed in the classroom. To promote equality among the races, both the positive and negative aspects of European and African history must be presented in an equal manner. That is not the situation today. Today's education focuses on the positive aspects of European history and the negative of African history which gives the false impression that Europeans are better than Africans. That false impression, among other factors, has caused huge financial, social and political gaps between the black and white races. Feel free to visit Department of Labor, Department of Education, National Center for Education Statistics, U.S. Census Bureau and Department of Health and Human Services websites for gap statistics. The Current Population Survey which is a joint project between the Bureau of Labor Statistics and Bureau of the Census Technical Paper 63 provides excellent data on achievement gaps. The wage and achievement gaps in America are perpetuated by the manner which Americans are taught. By exaggerating Europeans' accomplishments and masking their failures a high expectation for European success and a low expectation for European failure are created. By exaggerating Africans' failures and masking their accomplishments a high expectation for African failure and a low expectation for African success are created. In order to close these wage and

5

achievement gaps, these false impressions must be corrected via a balanced education to change the expectation. In order to balance education, more negative aspects of European history and positive aspects of African history must be presented in the classroom. Currently, most African Americans and European Americans are oblivious to the fact that savage and totally uncivilized Europeans existed. They are programmed to believe that the Europeans' history is rich and refined. In fact, the mention of a savage European will most likely bring scoffs, loathing and plenty of dirty looks, but that side of history does exist and must be faced. All people and all cultures of this world have both positive and negative aspects to their history. In order to promote true equality among people, both the positive and negative historical aspects must be presented equally in both quantity and quality, otherwise known as a true and full history. For African Americans to gain the confidence needed to achieve total physical, psychological, and mental freedom and advance their financial, social and political position to proper levels, they need their history education properly balanced. As Mr. Booker T. Washington recognized years ago, the balancing of the African Americans' ancestry education will brighten the path to knowledge of self, and ultimately allow them to realize the benefit of their ancestry in forwarding their race, the same as European Americans have. Currently, all are programmed not to even ponder the FACT that African Americans are the descendants of pharaohs, the original Fathers of Civilization, but now is the time to change. People of African descent, particularly African Americans, must acquire knowledge of themselves and then use the knowledge of themselves to demand respect from other races of the world instead of begging others to treat them equally, which they have been doing since Lincoln signed the Emancipation Proclamation.

The purpose of this text is to examine the current unbalanced nature of today's education and demonstrate how it

Knowledge of Self

prompts the utmost respect for people of European descent and lack of respect for people of African descent. This text is meant to expose how today's education subliminally deceives, brainwashes, hoodwinks and bamboozles all who are subjected to it. The ultimate goal is to provide you instruction on how you can properly balance the education of yourself and your children, which will promote the proper respect of people of African descent based on their worldly accomplishments instead of the pity and piousness of other races. The historical facts presented in this text will serve as starting blocks in your race towards knowledge of self thusly improving your cultural self-esteem. Begin the balancing process and introduce yourself to the concept of a true and full history.

2. *The Force*

There is an intangible force that currently perpetuates the concept of white superiority and black inferiority. The same force that subconsciously instructs African Americans to feel inferior because of their dark face, wide nose and full lips simultaneously injects a feeling of supreme superiority in whites due to the brightness of their skin, aquiline nose and thin lips. This force that makes people, black, white and every other color in between, assume Africa is a continent full of AIDS stricken wild men, is the exact same force that makes people automatically assume Europe is a continent full of esteemed, formal and proper gentlemen. This force also plays a role in the assumption that a black man in a big expensive car is a drug dealer, and a white man in the exact same car is a go-getter, young professional advancing his way up the corporate ladder. This is not some natural force God instilled in all of his children as no man, woman or child is born to hate oneself, or feel oneself inferior to another. This force is something that is learned. This force is common with calculating consistency across all color lines instilling the age old adage 'niggas and flies, the things I despise' in all people, not only people of African descent. It is relentless in drilling the myth of African American inferiority in all who are subjected to it. What could it be? What force is so powerful that it has conditioned a country of people to directly correlate shiny dark skin, short kinky hair, a wide nose and big lips as negative ugly physical characteristics of niggers? What force is so powerful that it has conditioned a country of people to directly correlate white skin, long straight blond hair and blue eyes as features of the beautiful people of the world? What force? What force convinces European and African Americans alike that people of African descent in America are an ignorant people who belong in the ghetto? What force is so powerful that it creates an automatic European American reflex to move out of their neighborhood when African Americans move in; clutch a pocketbook when a young African American male enters the area; and at the same time feel sorrow for the pitiful people of the city? What force creates a stigma that people of African descent are uneducated, uncivilized, barbaric niggas who deserve to be locked up? What force?

Could this force be the general American culture which is made up of many mini-cultures that exist within the United States? Mini-cultures within American culture vary greatly, far too greatly to create the consistency of black inferiority that exists today. There is simply too great a variation of what individual family members of individual racial groups explicitly or implicitly teach their children at home to create such a universal equation as African American = inferior humanity. For example:

One set of white parents may give their children a one time speech that God made all men equally, regardless of race, and that all men should be respected equally.

While.....

...another white parent who is a member of the Klu Klux Klan may be teaching his children that niggers are the

The Force

scum of the earth and should be spat upon on sight.

or

A set of black parents may consistently tell their kids that the black man is the supreme being, father of world civilization and should be respected as such.

While....

...another set of young black siblings may overhear their single black mother in a phone conversation with her girlfriend stating that 'niggas ain't no good'.

or

One set of Italian American parents may decide to tell their children about the great African General Hannibal and how he marched on Rome and left over 10,000 of his African troops in Italy to procreate with the Italian women, therefore deriving the source of their tinted white skin. [1]

While...

...another Italian American father may tell his only daughter 'never go out with a nigger, they're lazy and beneath you'.

From these examples, what each individual person within each individual mini-culture may be taught at home varies too greatly for culture to be this great force that seems to automatically deem blacks as inferior.

As stated earlier, this negative aura of inferiority of people of African descent is not something that is God given. It is something that is imposed on all people of society and reinforced to the point where the victim of the force becomes conditioned. The force subliminally teaches everyone that blacks are nothing. The force is not tangible, you can't touch it. The force is very sly. It teaches blacks to subliminally hate themselves even before they learn to read. The force was developed during a time in a very low point in the history of people with dark skin. What is this force that has continued the enslavement of the majority of the

11

black mind even some 140 years after physical slavery was officially abolished? What force could influence an entire population of an entire country in such a consistent manner? YOUR FORMAL AMERICAN AND WORLD HISTORY EDUCATION![2]

Your formal education, the very thing that is absolutely necessary for you to prosper in life, is the exact same thing that has successfully contained, entrapped and yes, enslaved the collective minds of African Americans while simultaneously providing psychological empowerment to the European American mind. Through words, sounds and pictures during at least the first eighteen years of your life, you were consistently taught in a subliminal manner that the worth of a black-skinned person is far less than the worth of a white-skinned person. World and American History courses in the United States consistently portray and describe blacks as expendable savages, un-human beings who were either naked running aimlessly in the jungles of Africa or half-clothed and obediently laboring in the American fields of the all-mighty master. Even the dictionary which is one of the most basic educational tools subliminally states that whites are better than blacks by the definitions printed for each. Go and actually look up the word 'black' in any dictionary and read the definitions. Merriam Webster defines black as very dark in color; dirty, soiled; characterized by the absence of light; thoroughly sinister or evil: wicked; indicative of condemnation or discredit; connected with invoking the supernatural and especially the devil; very sad, gloomy, or calamitous; marked by the occurrence of disaster; characterized by hostility or angry discontent. Then look up the word 'white'. Merriam Webster defines white as of the color of new snow or milk; from the former stereotypical association of good character with northern European descent; marked by upright fairness; free from spot or blemish; free from moral impurity; innocent; not intended to cause harm; favorable, fortunate.

The Force

The force in the form of your history classes has an overarching power that affects all subjected to it. Many are touched by the force without ever realizing it. If you have ever done any of the following acts, then you have fell victim to the power of the force:

- If you have ever referred to any person of color as a nigga, nigger, or however you want to spell it (even if you are black)
- If you have ever used the phrase 'niggas and flies, the things I despise' (again, even if you are black)
- If you have ever used the term 'forget that nigga' or 'forget 'em, they're just niggas'
- If in a professional setting, you have ever thought to yourself 'what are they doing in here' whenever a person of African descent walks into the meeting room
- If you have ever made the assumption that a person of color with expensive material possessions was a drug dealer
- If you have ever been shocked to see a person of African descent in any professional position of power
- If you have ever fought for racial segregation
- If you have ever felt the impulse to move out of a neighborhood just because blacks moved in
- If you have ever clinched your pocketbook just because you come into proximity to a young black male
- If you have ever locked your car door just because you come into proximity to a young black male
- Any black that ever moved out of the way of a white person or let a white get in front of them simply because that person was white
- Any white that expected to get in front of a black simply because they were black

The Force

- If you ever showed a general lack of respect towards a person of color simply because they were a person of color, then you have been affected by the force

Expression of any of these scenarios demonstrates how the force has directly affected you.

The general lack of respect for people of African descent stems from the academic stigma that people of African descent do not deserve respect due their published lowly place in history. The constant portrayal of African American forefathers in inherently inferior positions has crippling psychological affects on the current population of African Americans. While many blacks will verbally deny any feeling of inferiority ('I'm not inferior to anyone'), especially towards whites, their true feelings come to light when they beg European Americans to treat them fairly and beg to be their equals. If they didn't feel inferior, then why would they ask to be treated equally? The fact of the matter is European Americans will not be able to consider African Americans as equals until the history of African Americans and people of African descent is presented in the same manner as the history of Europeans Americans and people of European descent. The force throws off the balance of today's education, which creates a financial, social and political imbalance of society. As long as the force unbalances education, there will be no equality among the European American and African American cultures. In order to achieve equality, a positive force must be created to negate the negative force, but until that time the negative force as described in this section will continue to perpetuate the concept of black inferiority and white superiority, thusly perpetuating unequal financial, social and political positions between people of European American and African American cultures.

Part B: *Perspective & History*

The mind of several generations of Europeans would thus be gradually indoctrinated, Western opinion would crystallize and instinctively accept as revealed truth the equation: Negro=inferior humanity.[1]

Dr. Cheikh Anta Diop

3. *Perspective*

History (his-tu'-ree) as defined by Merriam-Webster is "a chronological record of significant events (as affecting a nation or institution) often including an explanation of their causes . . . a branch of knowledge that records and explains past events."[1] Hyperdictionary defines history as "the discipline that records and interprets past events involving human beings."[2] The consistency between both of these definitions is the discipline of history allows for a particular historian's documentation of past events and more importantly their <u>interpretation</u> and <u>explanation</u> of those events. When a person interprets and explains an event, they have the control to stress certain pieces of the event and downplay other pieces of the event. Quite naturally, a person's interpretation or explanation of any event, object or historical fact will be subject to the uniqueness of their individual perspective. A person's perspective is developed based on their life's experiences, their environment and their education. The nature of a person's experience, environment and education will have a direct affect on their perspective, which in turn will directly

Perspective

influence how that person interprets and explains historical facts. See Figure 1.

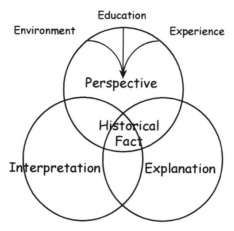

Figure 1 A person's interpretation and explanation of historical facts are directly affected by their perspective. A person's perspective is directly affected by their environment, experiences and education.

Let's examine the affect of perspective on the historical fact that Rodney King was beat to a pulp by the Los Angeles Police Department (L.A.P.D.). A 40 year old black man, who grew up in the inner city, with a high-school education and had been pulled over by the police 6 times in the last 6 months will interpret and explain the Rodney King beating entirely different than a 40 year old white male, who grew up in suburbia U.S.A., received an Ivy League education from Harvard and has never been pulled over by the police. Even though both of these gentlemen may have witnessed the exact same event on the exact same news cast on the exact same day, on the exact same TV, they will interpret and explain the event from separate ends of the spectrum based on their individual perspectives as directly influenced by their separate environments, education, and experiences.

Perspective

The 40 year old black gentleman was born and raised in the ghetto, surrounded by concrete, abandoned buildings and pot-hole ridden streets where he remains today as a man. He has a high school education, and has been pulled over by the police on his way to and from his job on numerous occasions without reason. From his perspective, the police are a nuisance, harassers and an overall threat to his livelihood as they constantly make him late for work. He also views the police as a threat to his health as their constant harassment causes him great stress. Not only did the man experience first hand harassment from the police, but as a child he also witnessed the police harass his older brother and father on a regular basis. As a result of his environment, education and experience, he interprets the Rodney King beatings as police brutality in its ultimate form, a form he fears he may one day face. Based on the affects of his environment, education and experience as described above, he explains that Mr. King was pulled over and beat for no apparent reason, just as he himself had been pulled over for no apparent reason so many times in the past.

The perspective of the 40 year old white gentlemen is quite different than the perspective of the black gentleman. The white gentleman grew up in suburbia U.S.A., surrounded by perfectly manicured green lawns and clean streets. After completing a Master's program at Harvard, he decided to buy a 4,000 square foot home in his childhood neighborhood. Regardless of his constant speeding in his sports car, he has never been pulled over by the police for any reason. As a child, he witnessed police pulling over young African American youths on their way from their ghetto to his suburbs. He gained a great appreciation for the police for protecting his neighborhood from those hoodlums as he figured they were up to something. Due to his environment, education and experience he interprets and explains the Rodney King beatings from his own unique perspective, very different from that of the black man in Figure 2.

Perspective

Rodney King Beating

Figure 2 The affects of perspective on a black man's interpretation and explanation of a historical fact (the Rodney King beating).

Rodney King Beating

Figure 3 The affects of perspective on a white man's interpretation and explanation of a historical fact (the Rodney King beating).

Perspective

The white man interprets and explains that Rodney King was up to no good just like those young hoodlums from his childhood who were attempting to pay a sneaky visit to his squeaky clean neighborhood. He interprets the beating as a simple case of the police protecting the citizens with the explanation of 'well, he shouldn't have broken the law'.

The perspective of the black gentleman portrayed in Figure 2 is quite different than the perspective of the white gentleman portrayed in Figure 3. Each individual interprets the vicious police beating of Rodney King quite differently from their individual perspectives.

$3a.$ *Individual Perspective & History*

The influence of perspective as described in the preceding chapter applies to all aspects of life, <u>including the discipline of history</u>! All historians participate in the discipline of history from their particular perspective. In other words, historical facts are interpreted and explained to others from the historian's particular point of view. There are thousands of history books in existence. All of these books interpret and explain the same historical facts, but they do so from each author's Individual Perspective. The individual interpretation and explanation from a particular perspective is what makes each history book unique. If these books were not unique interpretations and explanations of the same historical facts based on each author's perspective, then every history book would be the same, a simple statement of historical facts. There are thousands of history professors in the nation, and no two teach a course exactly the same. Every historian teaches history from his particular Individual

Individual Perspective & History

Perspective, which makes each class different despite the fact that they cover the same historical data.

Due to the influence of perspective on interpretation and explanation, the student must begin to consider the Individual Perspective of the teacher while learning history; the reader must begin to consider the perspective of the author; and the audience must begin to consider the perspective of the speaker. More specifically, the student, reader and audience must always consider the potential affect the teachers', authors' and speakers' perspective may have on their particular interpretation and explanation of historical facts. Many variables will affect the perspective of a historian. Factors such as:

- What was the historian taught as a child?
- Did his/her father constantly use racial slurs in the child's presence?
- Was the only interaction a white history teacher ever had with blacks when her purse was snatched downtown?
- Was the author of a series of history books the only white kid in an all black neighborhood?
- Was the author of a series of history books the only black kid in an all white neighborhood?
- Was a history professor taught ancient Egyptians were white?
- Was a history professor taught ancient Egyptians were black?
- Was the father of a southern historian lynched in Jim Crow Mississippi?
- Was the father of a northern historian killed in a 60's riot?
- Did the mother of a professor constantly refer to her and her siblings as little niggers?

Various facets of a historian's experience, education and environment will affect their perspective, and their perspective

Individual Perspective & History

will influence the way they interpret and explain anything, especially historical facts.

3b. *Group Perspective & History*

While no two individual's perspectives of all historical events are exactly the same, they can be very similar. For the most part, the perspective of those people who share similar experiences, have common education and were subject to the same or similar environment will be closely grouped together. In other words, people who share the same culture ·and environment will often times share a similar perspective. Note they will not be exactly the same but they will be closely grouped, with the exception of some anomalies of course. The perspective of people who share the same culture becomes related due to their similar experience, education and environment but note that it is not exact because their experience, environment and education are not exact. See Figure 4 below for a pictorial view on how perspectives can be related but not exact for people who have similar or common experiences, education and environment or who share a common culture:

27

Group Perspective & History

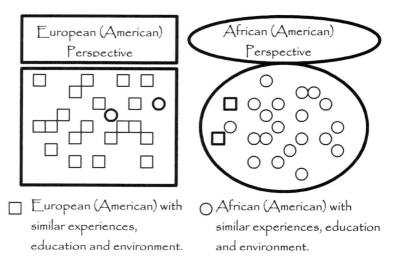

European (American)
Perspective

African (American)
Perspective

☐ European (American) with
  similar experiences,
  education and environment.

○ African (American) with
  similar experiences, education
  and environment.

Figure 4 Portrayal of how people with similar experiences, education and environment will have closely related perspectives.

Note there will be some anomalies where African Americans share the European American perspective due to commonality of the American culture and interaction between the cultures. For the most part, African Americans participating in the African American culture will share the African American Group Perspective. For example, most African Americans thought the Rodney King beatings were wrong. Similarly, there will be some anomalies where European Americans share the African American Group Perspective due to commonality of the American culture and interaction between the cultures. For the most part European Americans participating predominantly in the European American culture will share the European American Group Perspective i.e. most European Americans thought O.J. Simpson was guilty.

3c. *The Dominant Perspective*

World History as taught in the United States is dominantly interpreted and explained from the European American Group Perspective. This interpretation and explanation of select historical facts by people with similar education, experience, and environment is the source of today's unbalanced, one-sided, biased education. Etymology is the history or study of the source of a word and the etymology of the word 'history' is European as it is derived from the Greek word historia. In other words, even the word 'history' is European. The European and European American Group Perspective is the one that was portrayed to you during your elementary, middle, and high school education. The European American Group Perspectives was also portrayed to you during your higher education in modern day colleges and universities. The European and European American perspective is the most dominant because European and European Americans are the most financially, politically and socially powerful group in the modern world. Driven by a natural impulse for self-preservation they instinctively use their financial and political pull to portray

29

The Dominant Perspective

their ancestors in the most majestic fashion fathomable. European Americans control the curriculum and the process of teaching all Americans - white Americans, black Americans, Chinese Americans, etc. The majority of teachers are European American; the majority of school counselors are European American[1]; the majority of school principals are European American; most of the members of the Board of Education are European American; most of the employees of the Department of Education are European American; almost all members of Congress are European American; and the President is European American! Since eighty-two percent (82%) of the American population is European American, the European American Group Perspective of history must be the Dominant Perspective.[2] In fact, today's History courses should be named what they are - History from the Dominant European Perspective!

Since history is portrayed from the Dominant European and European American Perspective, it focuses on the history of Europeans and European Americans and their relationships with other people of the world. Of all the non-European people of the world, Africans and people of African descent have the oldest and most intimate link with Europeans. Consequently, the history of the Africans and African Americans is unfortunately portrayed from the Dominant European Perspective while the historical portrayal of other non-Europeans and non-European Americans becomes an after thought.

Fortunately, history is also interpreted from another, although not as dominant, perspective. African and African American historians, authors, activists and philanthropist do interpret and explain World History from an African and African American perspective. The African and African American perspective is not nearly as dominant as the European and European American perspective as African people and people of African descent are **no longer** the dominant culture in the world

30

The Dominant Perspective

(you will find out later in this text exactly why the phrase NO LONGER is used). Not only are they no longer the most dominant culture in the world, but they have also endured European and American slavery, imperialism and overall domination since Cambyses II conquered ancient Egypt about 525 B.C. Let's take a look at the discipline of history as interpreted and explained from the Dominant European and European American Perspective and the not so dominant African and African American perspective. Essentially, these two perspectives equate to:

What You Were Taught	History from the European and European American perspective
What You Were Not Taught	History from the African and African American perspective

Let's take a look at two prominent historical figures to depict how the history discipline is affected by African and European American Group Perspectives. Malcolm X and George Washington are two men who fought for the upliftment of their people. Washington fought for political, financial and social independence of white Americans from the English and Malcolm fought for political, financial and social independence of black Americans from white Americans. Although black Americans eventually were able to reap the benefits of George Washington's efforts, the fact remains that George Washington did not fight for the independence of black Americans. He stilled owned slaves years after 1776. In fact, President Washington expressed his disregard for Negroes in the following letter to ship Captain Josiah Thompson:

31

The Dominant Perspective

Sir: With this Letter comes a Negro (Tom) which I beg the favour of you to sell, in any of the Islands you may go to, for whatever he will fetch, and bring me in return from him

> One Hhd of best Molasses
> One Ditto of best Rum
> One Barrl of Lymes, if good and Cheap
> One Pot of Tamarinds, contg. about 10 lbs.
> Two small Do of mixed Sweetmeats, abt. 5 lb. each.
> And the residue, much or little, in good old Spirits

[H]e is exceedingly healthy, strong, and good at the Hoe . . . which gives me reason to hope he may, with your good management, sell well, if kept clean and trim'd up a little when offerd for Sale.

I shall very chearfully allow you the customary Commissions on this affair, and must beg the favour of you (lest he should attempt his escape) to keep him handcuffd till you get to Sea. . .[3]

In general, both Malcolm X and George Washington fought for the liberation of their respective races from an oppressor. President George Washington succeeded in his task. Unfortunately for African Americans, Malcolm X was assassinated before he could complete his mission. The force has taught me that:

> President George Washington was a true patriot, one of the Founding Fathers of our great country, a man of honor, respect and courage who even as a child could not tell a lie and admitted to chopping down the cherry tree. A man who should be gazed upon with great admiration.

The Dominant Perspective

And...

Malcolm X was a militant, radical, revolutionary, rebellious and belligerent Negro who was justifiably gunned down because of his mutinous attitude towards his country.

The interpretation and explanation of these two historical figures are from the Dominant European Perspective. If you took a survey of European Americans, you will find that most will agree with the interpretation and explanation of these two men.[4] Since European Americans control the education process, this perspective is probably what you were taught about George Washington and Malcolm X in elementary, middle and high school, that is if you were taught anything about Malcolm X at all. Essentially, they represent the European American Group Perspective as reflected in the curriculum and textbooks of American classes. Due to European Americans similar education, experience and environment, particularly the fact that they are the intentional beneficiaries of Washington's work, they interpret and explain his actions as truly honorable. Due to European Americans similar education, experience and environment, particularly the fact that Malcolm X mentally attacked other European Americans for the freedom of African Americans, they interpret and explain Malcolm's actions as hate driven mutiny.

Now, there is another perspective on the interpretation and explanation of the actions of these two men. Due to similar education, experience and environment of African Americans, specifically the facts that George Washington did not fight the British on their behalf and was an active slave owner, they interpret and explain his actions as oppressive and repressive to blacks.[5] Since African Americans are the unintentional beneficiaries of Washington's work, they are more nonchalant and less passionate about his accomplishments, unlike the intentional European beneficiaries. It would be surprising to find

33

The Dominant Perspective

any African American enthusiastic about the accomplishments of any person responsible for their great-great-grandparents being cracked on the back with a bull-whip in Mt. Vernon, Virginia. Now, due to similar education, experience and environment, African Americans interpret and explain Malcolm X's actions as the virtuous and righteous proceedings of a savior. They understand that Brother Malcolm fought on their behalf for political, financial and social independence. The commonality of Africans Americans' experiences causes them to view Brother Malcolm as a guardian of their God-given rights and an African American patriot the same as European Americans view George Washington as an European American patriot.

Neutrally speaking, Malcolm X was no more or less revolutionary, belligerent, mutinous, etc. than George Washington. Both men fought for the liberation of their people from an oppressor. Due to the influence of perspective and a God instilled need of self-preservation, Malcolm's revolution is portrayed in a dungeon-like negative light while Washington's in a majestically positive light, both from the Dominant European Group Perspective. Because of perspective, Washington's revolution was portrayed as right while Malcolm's revolution was portrayed as wrong. Would it be un-American for African Americans to view George Washington as an oppressor since he actively participated in slavery?[6] No, it is not un-American, because African Americans are Americans too. It is however un-European American to view George Washington as an oppressor and since the European American perspective is the most dominant, depicting George Washington in a negative light seems to be un-American. Is it un-American for African Americans to view Malcolm X as a savior? No, it is not un-American. It is however un-European American, and since the European American perspective is the most dominant, depicting Malcolm X as a savior seems to be un-American. But in the name of truth and honesty, the same way it is un-European

The Dominant Perspective

American to depict George as a militant radical and Malcolm as a savior, it is un-African American to depict George as a savior (since he actively operated in the slave trade) and Malcolm as a militant radical (since he fought for African Americans). In a just and balanced education, both of these perspectives would be portrayed in a balanced manner to reveal the full history of Washington and the full history of Malcolm. Unfortunately, both sides are not widely portrayed because your formal education is biased, unbalanced and taught from the European American perspective, the Dominant Perspective.[7] See Figure 5 for depiction.

The American Perspective		
THE DOMINANT PERSPECTIVE		
	European American Perspective	African American Perspective
George Washington	a true patriot, one of the Founding Fathers of our great country; a man of honor, respect and courage who should be looked upon with great admiration	oppressive and repressive to blacks; active slave owner; responsible for their great-great-grandparents being cracked on the back with a bull-whip
Malcolm X	a militant, radical, revolutionary, rebellious and belligerent Negro who was justifiably gunned down because of his mutinous attitude.	fought on their behalf for political, financial and social independence; virtuous and righteous proceedings of a savior; African American patriot; guardian of their God-given rights

Figure 5 Both the European and African American perspectives make up the American perspective. By simply comparing the above interpretations and explanations with what you were taught, you can easily determine which perspective is the Dominant Perspective.

The Dominant Perspective

Here's another example. The experience, education and environment of a European American male named Billy raised in Mississippi in 1940 has thoroughly reinforced the belief that all blacks are low down, dirty, lazy, good for nothing niggers who do not amount to anything, never have, never will. Now, when Billy is presented with the archaeological evidence to prove that all men came from Africa and that Africa is the source of human civilization (to be discussed in detail later in this text), Billy will go straight to disbelief. His education, experiences and environment has taught him that blacks are not even good enough to eat at the same lunch counter as whites, let alone capable of developing civilization. Because of that, his perspective will allow him to interpret and explain that some white people *must* have gone to Africa or there were whites who lived in Africa and developed civilization for the Africans. Remember, according to his experience, education and environment, no black is capable of developing civilization (See Individual Perspective). To expand this example, the Group Perspective of 1940 European American Mississippians would yield the same or very similar interpretation and explanation as the group shared the same or a very similar environment, education and experiences. Meaning Billy and his peers will share the same or similar Group Perspective (See Figure 4). Now to take it one step further, if this Group Perspective is the Dominant Perspective, then what you have is Billy and his peers as members of the Mississippi Board of Education agreeing to actively teach everyone in the Mississippi Public Schools that whites developed civilization in Africa.

Remember, there is another perspective! The experience, education and environment of an African American male named John in New York in 1940 has taught him that Africa is the proper homeland for all people of African descent since he has closely followed the teachings of prominent African Americans such as Marcus Garvey, Henry Highland Garnett,

The Dominant Perspective

Martin R. Delany and James Forten. He has read their speeches, studied their books and participated in their African American financial, political and social empowering practices. John is adamantly afro-centric and has a powerful sense of black pride, which in the 1940's would have been Negro pride. Now, when John is presented with the archaeological evidence to prove that all men came from Africa and that Africa is the source of civilization, he feels an immense sense of internal synchronization as if that was the last piece of a puzzle needed for wholeness. John's experience, education, and environment, primarily Marcus Garvey's teachings have reinforced a sense of self-worth in John and discovering all people came from his people, closes his loop. John's perspective as influenced by his experience, education and environment, specifically the influence of Marcus Garvey on his life, allows him to interpret and explain the African source of civilization as a heavenly truth that all should embrace. Now, the Group Perspective of John and his peers who have also been influenced by the teachings of Marcus Garvey will allow them to interpret and explain the archaeological evidence of the African origin of civilization as proof of the Black Man's magnificence. Since they all would share the same or very similar experience, education and environment, they naturally would come to the same or similar conclusion (See Figure 4).

Now, the difference here between Billy's and John's Group Perspective, is that John's Group is not the dominant group. Consequently, John's Group Perspective while just as important as Billy's will not be actively taught to millions in the New York public school system. In fact, since Billy and his peers are more financially, politically and socially dominant in the entire country, their Group Perspective will be taught in Mississippi public schools, New York public schools and every other school district in the country, thusly overwhelming and alienating John, his group and their perspective that civilization was developed in

The Dominant Perspective

Africa by Africans. (The African Origin of Civilization concept will be more formally introduced in the next section and closely examined in What You Were Not Taught).

4. *What You Were & Were Not Taught*

Despite the level of formal education an individual attains, there are certain historical facts that all Americans are familiar with. The culmination of these highly publicized historical facts as presented in today's classrooms make up what you were taught. There also exists another set of historical facts that most Americans are not familiar with that represents the other side of history. These other historical facts are extremely important but unfortunately are not publicized and remain unendorsed in any mainstream history curriculum. The culmination of these extremely important, non-publicized, unendorsed historical facts make up what you were not taught (the African American perspective). The aggressive promotion of what you were taught coupled with the disregard and general ignoring of what you were not taught is the source of the deception in your formal education.

What You Were & Were Not Taught

Negative Aspects of European History

African and European Americans were taught the history of past European heroes and heroines as they are heavily promoted in just about any World History class in the country. The force is certain to drill into our minds vision of grandeurs and magnificent accomplishments of white-skinned people of the earth. You are very familiar with the accomplishments of Julius Caesar, all Britain's King Georges and all the numerous European conquests of the world. You were taught that Columbus 'discovered' America and was told of Hitler's blond-haired, blue-eyed superior race. You know of Alexander the Great's conquers in Africa, Emperor Constantine's deeds, and the Berlin Conference where Europeans divided up Africa among themselves. YES, WE KNOW!

Now, African and European Americans were not taught of the savage, uncivilized side of Europeans. The curriculum never mentioned various Roman Emperors' molestation and rape of young Roman boys nor of the customary European incest and inter-marrying between brothers, sisters, fathers, mothers, sons, daughters, aunts, uncles and cousins. There was no mention of Europeans traveling to Northern Africa for their education, nor of the standing European custom to eat their dead. The murderous, deceitful, homicidal, suicidal and dysfunctional aspects of European history that actually were covered in history class were miraculously transformed into classical literary tragedies rather than being honestly described. The fact that royal mothers murdered royal sons, royal brothers murdered royal sisters, royal wives murdered royal husbands, royal fathers murdered royal sons somehow got transformed into heartbreaking soap opera type stories during your professor's lecture instead of being told like it really was, genocide. (These topics will be more formally examined in the chapter titled What You Were Not Taught).

What You Were & Were Not Taught

Positive Aspects of African History

All Americans were taught the European perception that Africans are uncivilized savages who require the help of missionaries and overall direction from white people to act in a civilized manner. You learned of European imperialism over the African continent and how the great European countries divided up the so-called 'Dark Continent' among themselves with no regard for its indigenous inhabitants. You are familiar with the jungles, wild animals and the perceived wild black people of the African continent. You know of the poor nations of the land and were taught to envision Africa as a continent full of rickety huts occupied by half dressed children with bloated bellies due to famine and disease. You learned about the oppression of black Africans by whites via apartheid in South Africa, the capture of African 'savages' for the trans-Atlantic slave trade and how Nelson Mandela seemed to be the only educated honorable African on the face of the earth, but even he was a convict. You also were taught that ancient Egyptians were some mysterious lost people who came, built the pyramids and somehow disappeared into thin air. You received the concept that the pyramids were some mysterious wonders of the world, perhaps built by aliens, and had seeds of doubt sowed in your brains in respect to the accuracy of any historical justification of an ancient black Egyptian civilization. In fact, most of us were taught that the ancient Egyptians who lived in northern Africa were white.

What African and European Americans were not taught is that ancient Egyptians were black people who developed civilization in Africa. Despite all the archaeological evidence, our history teachers neglected to teach us about the magnificent Africans who developed civilization and graciously passed it on to then barbaric Europeans. You do not know of the history of these ancient Africans despite the fact that it happens to be etched in stone on pyramid and temple walls.[1] You are unfamiliar

41

with the rich distant past of the dark skinned people of the Earth. Particularly, you were not taught anything about the time in history when **AFRICAN CULTURE DOMINATED** what was known as **THE CIVILIZED WORLD** and lived at the very **TOP RANK OF HUMAN CIVILIZATION**. Few are aware of the time in history when **AFRICANS** created civilization in the fertile Nile Valley of Mother Africa and frequently conquered their then barbaric European and Asian neighbors. Not many have ever seen the numerous Egyptian bas-reliefs that depict Africans as superior to Europeans but certainly you have seen numerous pictures of white slave masters dominating blacks. You were not taught of this time period typically referred to as some lost civilization of ancient African mystery. A few Americans may be able to faintly recall the dark-skinned African pharaohs decorated in gold back in Mother Africa but most will not. In fact, many are under the misconception that these great Fathers of Civilization in Egypt, Africa were white. Some historians present preposterous cases that the ancient Egyptians, i.e. Africans, were actually dark skinned white people and totally separate from so-called Negro type Africans that populate the rest of the continent. This concept of white Egypt Africans was well publicized by Billy and the boys, mentioned in the example in the previous chapter. Obviously, the more politically, socially and financially powerful group were able to spread the 'white people in Africa' message far and wide. The train of thought that there were whites who moved to Africa and developed civilization in the Nile Valley still lingers today as proved in movies and television programs about ancient Egypt. The actors cast in the ancient African roles are mostly white, some mixed, or in some rare cases very light skinned African Americans. You never see velvety, deep, dark-skinned African Americans or Africans in these roles. Even the History channel presents these ancient Africans as a light skinned, kind of in between mixed race instead of pure African blooded people of the past. Why? Is it because this mysterious race of white-blacks lived in Africa during that period and has since disappeared? Is it because no dark skinned actors were available during taping to play these roles? Or is it because the writers and directors of these programs and movies of European descent fell victim to their human need of self-pride, self-esteem and self-worth and also victimized by the force, naturally wrote, directed and cast their films about the fathers of civilization from the Dominant European Perspective? As you will see later in this text, civilization was developed in the Nile River Valley of Egypt, Africa by <u>pure Africans</u>. You were taught that Africans in general were savage beings, uncivilized and unable to think for themselves. You were not taught of the magnificent Royal African Empires in Western Africa. You did not learn about the Mandingo Kingdom of Mali, Timbuktu, Songhay, their intricate universities, rich natural resources nor their contributions to world society. You were taught about European imperialism over Africa, but were not taught about the Africans physical, mental, social and political battles with the Europeans for their freedom, which by the way were all won by every African nation. You were not taught about the men who led these battles such as King Cetewayo, Emperor Menelik II, the Zulu's nor the Ashanti.

What you were taught is an unbalanced history. What you were not taught is the rest of the proverbial story that will allow you to attain true and full history. This knowledge of the true and full history of the people of the world will expose the deceit of your current education and create balance and equality between the black and white races. **UNTIL HISTORY EDUCATION IS BALANCED, THERE WILL NEVER BE TRUE EQUALITY BETWEEN THE RACES!** As long as we are taught:

➢ whites achieved higher accomplishments than blacks
➢ whites posses a richer history than blacks
➢ whites are more intelligent than blacks
➢ whites have always dominated blacks

What You Were & Were Not Taught

> ➤ whites brought civilization to 'savage' Africans etc.

there will never, ever be equality among people of European American and African American cultures. As long as we are all conditioned by education that whites are better than blacks, there will never be equality among them. There can not be equality if we are all subliminally taught that whites are better than blacks, which is exactly what we have been taught in America since its inception.

Part C: *World History, Perspective & Balance*

One thing that is so inconceivable to you, because of the success of massive propaganda, is that over half of human history was over before anyone knew that the European was in the world.[1]

Dr. John Henrik Clarke

5. *Unbalanced Nature of World History*

It is a widely agreed upon fact among historians and archaeologists that human life began in Africa. Enough ancient African artifacts have been founded and confiscated, for lack of a better word, by many noted archaeologist to thoroughly prove this point. One of the more famous of these discoveries is the founding of a 1.8 million year old humanoid skeleton named Zinjanthropus in East Africa by Drs. Louis S. B. and Mary Leakey in 1959. The remains were discovered by the couple in the Olduvai Gorge in what is now Tanzania, Africa. Other archaeologists have had numerous other African 'discoveries' to thoroughly prove where the roots of humanity lie, but you were not taught anything about them or their hardcore evidence such as: the Taung Child found in South Africa, dated 2.5M years old; Lucy found in Ethiopia, dated 3.2M years old; the Dikika Baby found in Ethiopia, dated 3.2M years old; and the Millennium Man found in Kenya, dated 6.0M years old. Despite the archaeological evidence, general education seems to dub the

Unbalanced Nature of World History

African origin of man as some dark mystery or far fetched controversial belief of back to Africa fanatics. Even the Smithsonian Museum of Natural History in Washington D.C. creates an heir of uncertainty by placing the following disclaimer at the beginning of its human evolution exhibit:

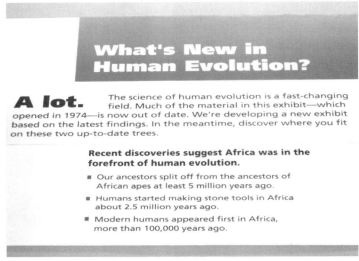

Figure 6 Smithsonian Natural History Museum Human Evolution Exhibit disclaimer.

Now, the sign states that the human evolution exhibit opened in 1974. By 1974 several noted archaeologists including the Drs. Leakey had made their discoveries of hard skeletal evidence that PROVED humans originated in Africa. For some unknown reason, the hard skeletal evidence only 'suggest Africa was in the forefront of human evolution' instead of proving Africa is the home of human origin. But the exhibit is admittedly out of date and hopefully whenever it is updated, it will account for factual evidence documented over 60 years ago in 1959.

Despite archaeological evidence and the overall concurrence between educators, historians, scientists, archeologists and other experts in the field of human origin, the

48

Unbalanced Nature of World History

fact that Africa is the birthplace of all mankind somehow remains unknown to general society. Educators at best reluctantly admit or passively deny the fact that human life began in Africa millions of years ago by claiming more research needs to be done. This documented fact should be proactively preached the same way the *belief* Christopher Columbus discovered America is proactively preached. On cue, a group of above-average, average, and below average educated individuals can rhyme in unison the belief 'In fourteen hundred ninety-two, Columbus sailed the ocean blue', because that historical concept is proactively preached in every elementary school across the country. However, there is no equivalent dedication on behalf of educators to proactively preach the historical fact that Africa is the origin of man. A method of aggressively publicizing this truth can be as simple as the rhyme 'Millions of years ago, the first man on Earth in Mother Africa began to grow'. But it is not, because your world history education is unbalanced.

Obviously and very logically, where world's first man was born (Africa), the world's first civilized culture (African Culture) developed the world's first civilization (African Nile Valley Civilization). Contrary to the strange interpretation and explanation of some historians who thought the ancient Egyptians were white, they were not. Ancient Egyptians were Africans, black with beautiful big lips and prominent wide noses. All cultures of the world have what many historians and social studies professionals refer to as a period of civilization. This period of civilization is a general period in time in the history of a people where they begin to exhibit characteristics of civilized behavior such as writing, commerce, government structure, religion, culture, arts, sciences, etc. As determined in the earlier chapter, each historian's interpretation and explanation of a historical event or artifact will be subject to the uniqueness of their Individual Perspective. Since each historian, professor or researcher interprets and explains historical events and artifacts

49

in accordance with their Individual Perspective, published periods of civilization for both the black skinned and white skinned people of the world vary. Given the lack of documentation from ancient Africans and Europeans that specifically state 'our culture became civilized on this day of this year', it is the historians' responsibility to interpret and explain historical facts and artifacts that document the period of time each culture became civilized. Now remember none of these historians were present then, so the best they can do is provide educated guesses. Therefore, it is our responsibility to analyze the historians' interpretations and explanations (best guesses) and decide what is logical and what is illogical.

According to the great historian and Egyptologist Dr. Yosef ben-Jochannan, ancient Egyptian High Culture i.e. High Civilization in Egypt, Africa began with the unification of the Northern pre-dynastic Egyptian Kingdom and the Southern pre-dynastic Nubian Kingdom under Pharaoh Menses (a.k.a. Pharaoh Aha or Narmer) around 3200 B.C.[1] This unification represents the first formal Dynasty of African History as defined by the Egyptian High Priest Manetho. This complex unification of two separate African Kingdoms, two separate governments and social structures under one pharaoh represents a very complex African civilization. But, before you get to a complex, high civilization, just plain old civilization must be attained. Therefore, it is logical to conclude that in order for there to have been two separate established African Kingdoms in 3200 B.C. for Pharaoh Menses to unify, Africans must have exhibited characteristics of a civilized society thousands of years before 3200 B.C. In fact, the esteemed Professor John G. Jackson in his book *Introduction to African Civilizations* notes that a group of Africans in "Lower Egypt had sixty kings before the reign of Menes [Menses]" and "[e]ven in predynastic times the Egyptians had reached a high level of civilization."[2] The Minnesota State University eMuseum identifies the Egyptian civilized pre-dynastic period as early as 7000 B.C. – 4950 B.C. where the "main constituents of civilization of unified Egypt were gradually introduced."[3] Dr. Cheikh Anta Diop very logically derived that nature forced the early inhabitants of the Nile River Valley in Africa to work, communicate and build together, which perpetuated the development of civilization in this area.[4] Dr. Diop professes the annual flooding of the Nile River forced the ancient Africans to survive and rebuild together what the river had destroyed, the same as Americans in the mid-west who experience flooding are forced to work together to survive and rebuild. The annual flooding of the Nile River perpetuated the development of civilization in the continent where the first man was born, Africa. So, for the sake of argument, particularly argument with those who have been brainwashed by the force, the remainder of this text will conservatively refer to the period of African civilization as 7000 B.C. - 5000 B.C., even though some sources note African civilization occurring as early as 10,000 B.C. with the Sebilian, Faiyum, Tasian and Badarian African cultures.

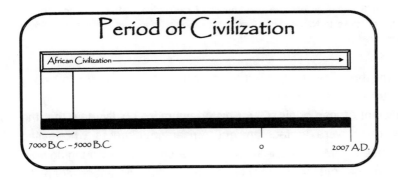

Figure 7 The period when Africans became civilized.

The first traces of civilization in Europe appeared in the form of the Minoan culture on the island of Crete. If you take a

51

look at a map, you will notice that the Crete Island is situated very closely to the birthplace of civilization, northeast Africa.

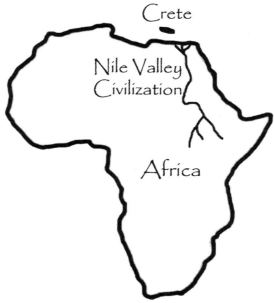

Figure 8 Crete, where the first traces of civilization in Europe appeared, is situated close to Nile Valley Africa, where the first traces of civilization in Africa appeared.

After the analysis and study of ancient Minoan artifacts, many historians have interpreted and explained them as having an ancient African origin. Other historians more boldly state that the Minoans were in fact ancient African immigrants who sailed across the Mediterranean Sea to the small island bringing with them the gift of civilization from Africa. Professor John G. Jackson specifically states that "[t]he ancestors of the Cretans were natives of Africa, a branch of the western Ethiopians. They dwelt in the grasslands of North Africa before that area dried up and became a great desert. As the Saharan sands encroached

52

on their homeland, they took to the sea, and in Crete and neighboring islands set up maritime culture."[5] This interpretation seems very logical since ancient Africans were the first to develop the boat, ancient Cretans wrote in African hieroglyphics, and especially since wall paintings such as Figure 9 depicting chocolate skinned Minoans still remain on the walls of ancient Crete structures.

Figure 9 Wall painting from Minoan Palace of Knossos depicting dark-skinned Minoans carrying fresh game.

Again, due to the varying perspectives of different historians and archaeologist, the period of Minoan civilization varies. This text will consider 3000 B.C. – 2000 B.C. the period of Minoan civilization. Unfortunately, the Minoan civilization did not last very long as they were invaded by barbarians from Northern Europe, the Mycenaeans. The Mycenaeans are estimated to have crushed the Minoans about 1500 B.C and they are the ancestors of Europeans. The Mycenaeans who hailed from Northern Europe spoke primitive Greek and are believed to be the indigenous ancestors of traditional white-skinned Europeans. The Mycenaeans are interpreted and explained as barbaric, illiterate, war-like uncivilized people from the North who finally became civilized using the remains of the Minoan culture about 1300 B.C. – 1200 B.C.[6] If for whatever reason, you believe the chocolate Minoans pictured in Figure 9 to be Europeans, then the period of European civilization is 3000 B.C. - 2000 B.C., otherwise the period of European civilization is with the Mycenaeans between 1300 B.C. – 1200 B.C. Since it seems more logical that the dark-skinned Minoans were actually Africans who migrated into Crete, the remainder of this text will conservatively refer to the period of European civilization as 1300 B.C. - 1200 B.C with the Mycenaeans.

Now if you compare the latest possible point of African civilization (5000 B.C.) and the earliest possible point of European civilization (1300 B.C.) you will find that Africans were civilized at least 3,700 years before Europeans showed even traces of civilization, yes that's three thousand seven hundred years! See Figure 10 below:

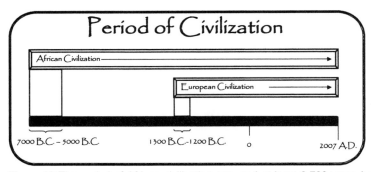

Figure 10 The period of African civilization occurred at least 3,700 years before European civilization.

Regardless of all the archaeological evidence founded by European archaeologists, the concept of Royal Egyptian Africans creating civilization, developing writing, establishing government and social structures, developing commerce, etc. while ancient Europeans wandered icy Europe in barbarism was never taught. The concept of black-skinned, full lipped Africans managing the design, development and construction of

Unbalanced Nature of World History

monstrous pyramids while white-skinned barbarians of Europe killed each other for food was totally ignored. Unfortunately, African Americans are taught their African history by European American teachers, books and administrators with a sometimes deviant focus on the history of the world after the point of European civilization. The fact that the point of African civilization had occurred 3,700 years before the point of European civilization is completely ignored. They teach the history of the world from the dominant European Perspective. In *Black Man of the Nile* Dr. Yosef ben-Jochannan explains by the time the first white "arrived in Northeast Alkebu-lan [Africa], at Ta-Merry [Egypt], about 1675 B.C.E., . . . the indigenous Africans . . . had already developed most of their Nile Valley High-Cultures, and were in the midst of their XIVth Dynasty in Ta-Merry [Egypt], Ta-Nehsi [Nubia],and Ethiopia."[7] Africans were the first to write, sensibly speak, build, trade, negotiate, farm, fish, sail, rule, unify, organize, pray, preach, invent, form, develop, manage, lead, etc. some 3,700 years before any European exercised basic hygiene.

The focus of historians on history after the point of European civilization is a primary cause of your biased education. Of the first 7,007 years of the history of civilized man (5000 B.C. to 2007 A.D.), you were only taught half the story (1300 B.C. to 2007 A.D.). For example, an individual with an average education would know much more about the Roman Empire which lasted only about 500 years beginning with Julius Caesar around 27 B.C. than they would know about any of the Egyptian Dynasties which lasted for about 3,000 years beginning with Pharaoh Menses in 3200 B.C, 3,173 years before the Roman Empire even existed. If you do not believe it, then conduct a simple survey of 10, 50, or even 200 people. Ask them if they know of Julius Caesar, then ask those same people if they know of Pharaoh Menses and feel free to send me your results at nqc@knowledgeofselfpublishing.com. In the end what you will find is regardless of the archaeological evidence and hundreds

Unbalanced Nature of World History

of books documenting the civilization of ancient Africans before Europeans, your formal history education conveniently ignored this period and focused primarily on history after the point of European civilization, which is a prime suspect in causing a great imbalance in your education. See below for depiction.

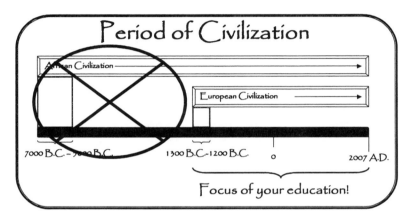

Figure 11 Your education focused on history after the period of European civilization.

Europeans and European descendents were taught the knowledge of themselves from the period of European civilization to date. Africans and African descendants were also taught the knowledge of themselves from the period of European civilization to date. The time period from European civilization to date has been financially, politically, intellectually and physically dominated by Europeans. Since your education focused on this time period and this time period only, the false picture is presented that Europeans and European descendants are totally dominant to Africans and African descendants. But if you look behind that picture (i.e. before the point of European civilization) you will note that exactly the opposite was true. You will see that the African culture dominated the period from African civilization

Unbalanced Nature of World History

to the period of European civilization. Once armed with the knowledge that Africans have dominated and ruled Europeans in the past i.e. Africans are capable of dominating and ruling Europeans, maybe you will begin to recognize that Africans and African descendants should be respected just as Europeans and European descendants. Maybe, just maybe, Europeans will truly accept African and African descendants as true equals on paper and in conduct.

6. *What You Were Taught (The Dominant Perspective)*

Let's run through a quick mental exercise to demonstrate exactly how your world history education was administered from a biased European perspective. This mental exercise will actively demonstrate that your formal world history education focused primarily on the positive achievements and supposed superiority of Europeans. It will also demonstrate that the majority of what you were taught of African history focuses on the negative aspects of African people and promotes a concept of African inferiority. For the time being, keep the focus on your world history education. Before beginning, please take a moment to digest the following three facts:

1) Civilization began in Africa.

2) Formal African Kingdoms with complex social structures, government, agriculture, language, etc. are documented by archaeological evidence to have existed as early as 5000 B.C.

59

What You Were Taught (Dominant Perspective)

3) Traces of the first basic European civilization
in Greece dates back only to about 1300 B.C.
which is 3,700 years after Africans had formed
formal kingdoms.

*All of these facts will be proven in the next
chapter, What You Were Not Taught.

With those facts digested, take a minute to think back through
your education with specific focus on your world history
education. Try to remember all you can about your history
education. Be sure to think all the way back to your elementary
school days. Recall any world history courses from middle and
high school. Remember all college level History 101 and 102
courses. Even recall history lessons embedded in other courses
such as Humanities, Social Studies or Religion. Try to envision
the classroom. Think of your fellow classmates and your
teachers. If you can, remember lesson plans, activity sheets and
syllabi. Try to picture your text books. If at all possible, visualize
the cover of the text books, the authors' names and their pictures
on the back cover. Try to recall pictures inside the textbooks.
Can you see any faces on the pages? Can you remember any
scenes? Think back, think hard. Recall the topics or even
chapter titles. What do you remember? Please take a couple of
minutes to recall all you can of your history education...

What topics are you able to recall? Which cultures can
you remember studying? Which countries do you remember
reading about? What did you read about them? What group of
people in the world do you remember discussing? What
individuals in the world do you remember studying? What time
periods? As I search through my memory, I can explicitly recall
the following:

Europe, vivid and beautiful pictures of European
kings and queens draped in velvet and gold,
Greeks and their growth and conquers, Iliad,
Odyssey,   Homer,   Socrates,   Aristotle,

What You Were Taught (Dominant Perspective)

Pythagoras, Pythagorean Theorem, Persians and all of their accomplishments, Persian Wars, Plato, Philosophy, Pericles, Alexander the Great[1], Herodotus, Cyrus, Darius, Macedonians and all of their accomplishments, Babylon, King Louis X, England, William Shakespeare, Hamlet, Romeo and Juliet, Mid Summersnight Dream, Buckingham Palace and its guards with the red coats and tall hats, Big Ben, Italy (the boot on the map), Rome, Roman Empire and all of its accomplishments, Sicily, Julius Caesar, Marc Anthony, Cleopatra, the Coliseum, leaning tower of Pisa, aqueducts, Spain, King Ferdinand, Queen Isabella, France, Napoleon, Portugal, Russia, U.S.S.R., Ivan the Terrible, Czars, Prussia, Scandinavian Peninsula, Norway, Sweden, Finland (the moose head), World War I, World War II, Germany, Hitler, blitzkrieg, all types of Agreements between European countries, Pearl Harbor, Japanese kamikaze pilots, Mongolia, China, Ming Dynasty, Japan, A-Bomb, Antarctica, Africa, Sahara Desert, South Africa, apartheid, Nile River, imperialism, natives, Gilgamesh, Communist Manifesto, Sigmund Freud, Constantine, Mythology, Athens, Sparta, Baghavad Gita, Ottoman Turks.

About 99% of the topics I can recall relate back to Europe and Europeans after the point of European civilization because all my peers and I were taught from a European perspective. The world history curriculum was developed primarily by European Americans. The world history textbooks we learned from were written primarily by European Americans. Despite the fact that I received my K-12 education in the inner city, the majority of my teachers were European American. The

61

What You Were Taught (Dominant Perspective)

school counselors were European American[2]. The principal was European American. Most of the members of the Board of Education were European American. Most of the employees of the Department of Education were European American. Almost all members of Congress were European American and the President was European American! To top it all off, all of these European Americans were taught themselves by European Americans (Billy and the boys!) also from the Dominant European American Perspective. To make matters worse, so were their teachers, and the teachers before them, who all were ultimately taught the history of the world by ancient Europeans from the Dominant European Perspective. The below figure provides a graphical representation of how my classmates and I in the inner city were taught from the European perspective. The **A** represents African history topics and the **E** represents European history topics listed in the previous paragraph.

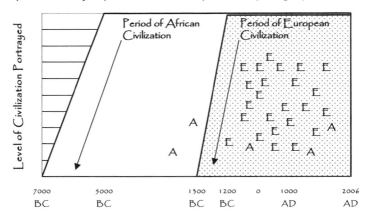

Figure 12 Our unbalanced education.

Please note, almost all of the topics mentioned tie back to world history after the point of European civilization. There were not many pre-European civilization topics covered because history

What You Were Taught (Dominant Perspective)

was taught from a European perspective. The graph clearly depicts the vast majority of historical topics covered were those about or directly related to the history of European peoples. The few African history topics covered were unfortunately taught as some negative, inferior relation to post-European civilization. For example, we learned how the leaders of European countries got together in Berlin, Germany in 1884 and divided up the continent of Africa among themselves, otherwise known as the Berlin Conference. We learned:

➤ of African heritage from the perspective of or in relation to European heritage. Since the magnitude of the European-African relationship post European civilization was abusive, we learned of how Africans were conquered and abused by Europeans.

➤ what Europeans thought about Africans instead of what Africans thought about Africans.

➤ how Europeans thought Africans were ignorant, uncivilized savages.

➤ about the history of Africans from the European perspective.

➤ too much about the positive side of European history and too little about the negative.

➤ too much about the negative side of African history and too little about the positive.

The majority of the un-proportional African history taught focused primarily on the negative aspects and little to none on the positive aspects of African history. The method of this strategic teaching would falsely lead one to believe that the history of the African is shallow, meager, pitiable and outright pathetic, while the history of the European is majestic, proud, stately and justifiably dignified. The consistent portrayal of past Africans as shallow, meager, pitiable and pathetic carries the psychological threat of influencing their descendants to embody these negative characteristics. The consistent portrayal of past Africans as inferior to past Europeans carries the psychological threat of influencing African descendants to feel inferior to European descendants. Unfortunately, this threat has been realized in the current American population. The consistent portrayal of past Europeans as majestic, proud, stately and justifiably dignified drives their descendants to embody these positive characteristics. Additionally, the consistent portrayal of past Europeans as superior to past Africans drives their descendants to feel and act superior to African descendants. Unfortunately, this threat has also been realized in the current American population. Herein lays the deception in your education. By only presenting half the story, you (be you black, white, orange, polka-dot) are deceived to believe Europeans/whites are better than Africans/blacks.

Take a second to analyze the data you were able to recall about your own education. Use the below template to graph the results of what you could recall. Use an **A** to denote African history topics and an **E** to reflect European history topics. Also be certain to place your **E**'s and **A**'s in the appropriate time period using the time scale at the bottom of the graph.

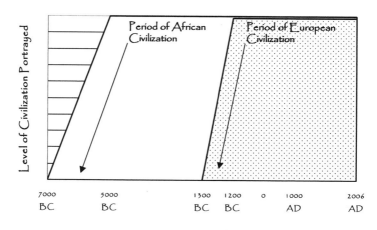

Figure 13 Your unbalanced education.

64

What You Were Taught (Dominant Perspective)

Does your graph look anything like ours? Certainly it does, because you were taught history from the Dominant European Perspective.

To really drive the point home, a further categorization of your unbalanced history is necessary. Each of the different topics listed must be categorized as presenting Europeans in a positive or negative light or as presenting Africans in a positive or negative light. Use the following symbols to perform your categorization: European Positive = **EP**, European Negative = EN, African Positive = **AP**, African Negative = **AN**. The below figure represents the further categorization of what my classmates and I learned:

	European History	African History
Positive	EP EP EP EP EP EP EP EP EP EP EP EP EP EP EP EP EP EP EP	AP
Negative	EN EN EN EN	AN AN AN AN AN AN AN AN AN AN

Figure 14 Further categorization of my unbalanced education.

Do you see the imbalance? Look closely and you will notice several imbalances as follows:

What You Were Taught (Dominant Perspective)

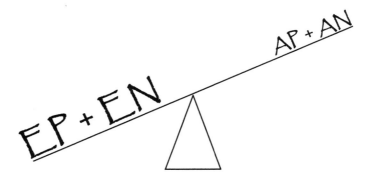

Figure 15 First, the total number of European topics taught (EP + EN), whether positive or negative, far outweighs the number of African topics (AP +AN), therefore creating an imbalance.

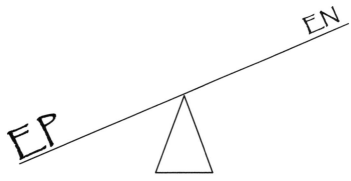

Figure 16 Next, please notice how many more positive aspects of the Europeans' history (EP) were presented, as compared with the negative (EN), therefore creating an imbalance.

What You Were Taught (Dominant Perspective)

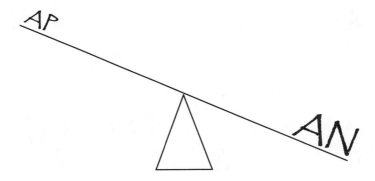

Figure 17 On the contrary, please notice how many more negative aspects of the Africans' history (AN) was presented, as compared to the positive (AP), therefore creating an imbalance.

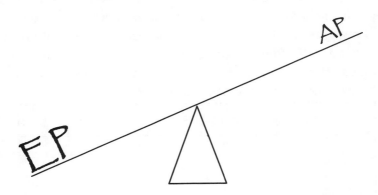

Figure 18 Next, note the number of topics which portray Europeans in a positive light (EP) far outweigh topics which portray Africans in a positive light (AP), therefore creating an imbalance.

What You Were Taught (Dominant Perspective)

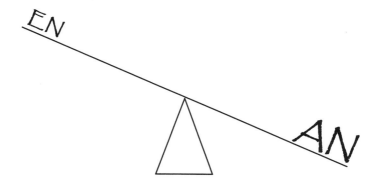

Figure 19 Lastly, please note the number of topics which portray Africans in a negative light (AN), far outweigh topics which portray Europeans in a negative light (EN).

Take a second to analyze the data you were able to recall about your own education. Categorize your data as presenting Europeans in a positive or negative light or as presenting Africans in a positive or negative light using the following symbols to perform your categorization: European Positive = **EP**, European Negative = **EN**, African Positive = **AP**, African Negative = **AN**. Map your data in the proper area on the below table. Do you see an imbalance?

	European History	African History
Positive		
Negative		

Figure 20 Further categorization of your unbalanced education.

What You Were Taught (Dominant Perspective)

Does your table look anything like ours? Again, certainly it does because like us you were taught history from a European perspective.

You were taught that the world's first historian, philosopher, author, sailor were all Europeans. Your history books claim that Herodotus, who lived about (500 B.C.), was the world's first historian. He was even given the moniker 'the Father of History'. But when the 'World's First Historian Award' was decided, no consideration was given to those ancient Africans who etched and painted their history on the walls of obelisks, ancient temples and pyramids.[3] Why? Simple, you were taught an imbalanced and partial history from a European perspective. In fact, this man Herodotus, who European historians proclaimed the 'Father of History', explicitly stated that the Egyptians were the first historians when he noted 2,500 years ago that "they cultivate [record] the memory of past events more than any other men" and "are the best informed of all with whom I have had intercourse [questioned]."[4] So why would Herodotus get the 'World's First Historian Award' if he himself wrote about African historians who preceded him? Skewed and unbalanced perspective is the answer.

You were taught that the world's first philosophers were the ancient Greeks: Socrates, Plato and Aristotle. But when the 'World's First Philosophers Award' was decided, no consideration was given to the ancient African priests who actually developed philosophy, taught it to the ancient Greeks, then had their former Greek students claim it for their own.[5] Why? Simple, you were taught an imbalanced and partial history from a European perspective.

You were taught that the world's first literary masterpiece was Homer's Iliad, despite the looming question of Homer's alleged plagiarism[6]. But, when the 'World's First Literary Masterpiece Award' was decided, no consideration was given to the ancient Africans who DEVELOPED THE WORLD'S FIRST

What You Were Taught (Dominant Perspective)

ALPHABET AND FIRST FORM OF WRITING (hieroglyphics) and penned the *Book of Coming Forth To Day From Night* on papyrus which predates Homer by thousands of years.[7] Why? Simple, you were taught an imbalanced and partial history from a European perspective. Hieroglyphics was the first form of writing, developed in Africa by ancient Egyptian Africans. It makes perfect logical sense that the people who developed writing would have created the world's first literary masterpiece. Instead of studying *The Iliad* and *The Odyssey* in English class, we all should have studied *Book of Coming Forth To Day From Night*, but we did not because that text is African and our education was taught from the European perspective.

You were taught that at one point in time EVERYBODY thought the world was flat and Christopher Columbus was the world's first navigator to prove that the world is round. But when the 'World's First Navigator to Prove the World is Round Award' was decided, no consideration was given to ancient Africans who sailed the ocean blue at least 4,100 years before Columbus' birth. No consideration was given to Pharaoh Khufu who had his own Solar Barge now located in the Cairo Museum (pictured and discussed later in this text). No consideration was given to any Africans of the Mali Empire who crossed the Atlantic years before Columbus.[8] No consideration was given to the African navigator Hano who circumnavigated the African continent about 600 B.C. which was about 2,000 years before Columbus was born.[9] Nor was any consideration given to any other ancient African who voyaged across the Atlantic and settled in Mexico, Caribbean Islands, territories in Central and South America as documented by numerous ancient artifacts with African features founded in those regions.[10] WHY?! Simple, you were taught an imbalanced and partial history from a European perspective. So when your elementary school teacher told you 'EVERYBODY' thought the world was flat before Columbus' plunders, she really meant every European thought the world was flat, as ancient

What You Were Taught (Dominant Perspective)

Africans already knew the world was round, and rotated in an orbit around the sun hundreds of years before 1492.[11] (An example of artifacts will be given later in this text, along with solid evidence to support all these facts).

This list of unconsidered African history could go on and on as there is about 3,700 years worth of it. The point is that the European people, the historians, the educators, the archaeologist, the doctors, the lawyers, the laborers, etc. who decided the 'World's First Awards' identified the victors along with hundreds of others from a European perspective. The previously listed awards are more properly described as the 'World's First European ... Awards', but the 'European' was left out as it is assumed in your basic education since your education was taught from the Dominant European Perspective. Only European contestants and accomplishments were considered, documented and passed on down the line from European educator to European educator to European educator administrator, straight into your curriculum.

What you were taught is a history of the world that is skewed and unbalanced in many dimensions. What you were taught about the history of the world is unbalanced because what you were taught:

1.   ...has its primary and secondary focus on the history of white people, while treating the history of black people (people of African descent) as an after thought. (**EP + EN** > AP + AN)

2.   ...concentrates on the conquers, achievements, dominations and other positive aspects of white people after their period of civilization while ignoring the barbaric, embarrassing, scandalous negative side of white people. (**EP** > EN)

3.   ...concentrates on the negative aspects of black history, specifically focusing on the period in time when Africans and people of African

descent were dominated by white people. (AP<**AN**)

4. ...presents a gross number of historical events that portray Europeans in a positive light and a miniscule number of historical events that portray Africans in a positive light. (**EP**>AP)

5. ...presents a gross number of historical events that portray Africans in a negative light and a miniscule number of historical events that portray Europeans in a negative light. (EN<**AN**)

6. ...totally ignores the period in history where blacks in ancient Egypt developed civilization and passed it on to barbaric whites of Europe.

Is it possible that the Europeans do not have many negative aspects to their history, where they conducted themselves in a barbaric manner on the bottom of civilization? Is it possible that African Americans are the descendants of only jungle savages and slaves and there really are not many positive aspects to their history? Is it possible that only Europeans are capable of invading and conquering Africans and Africans are not capable of invading and conquering Europeans? NO. The answers to these questions make up What You Were NOT Taught, covered in the next chapter.

7. *What You Were Not Taught (The Truth)*

Of the first 7,007 years of the history of civilized man, you were only taught half the story. If you have not learned the important principle 'there are two sides to every story' thus far in your life, prepare yourself for a lesson. If you have learned that principle, then please prepare yourself for a life-altering example. This chapter will look into the other side of history, what you were not taught. So far we have established that your history education unjustifiably focused on the positive portrayal of Europeans, the negative portrayal of Africans and exemplified a superior-inferior relationship between the two. The cause for this unbalanced depiction is directly related to the influence perspective has on any historian's interpretation and explanation of historical events. In other words, a historian's natural instinct to see themselves and their forefathers in a positive light coupled with the influence of perspective causes the either intentional or unintentional biased presentation of historical facts. Your history education consistently conditioned you and is currently conditioning your children to correlate magnificence and superiority with the European and their descendents and savagery and inferiority with the African and their descendents. The mental conditioning is so effective that the mere thought of a savage/inferior European and a majestic/superior African drives you directly to disbelief. But believe it or not, there is immense savagery, barbarism and inferiority that surround Europeans and European descendents manifested in uncivilized European actions. Believe it or not, there is great magnificence, pride and superiority that surround Africans and African descendants exemplified by cultured, educated and sophisticated acts of African pharaohs, kings, queens, priests, warriors, educators and citizens. But as demonstrated in earlier chapters of this text (What You Were Taught), your history education consistently focused on the positive aspects of European history and the negative aspects of African history, both after the point of European civilization. But the other side of history (What You Were Not Taught) focuses on the negative aspects of European history and the positive aspects of African history, after the point of African civilization to create **balance** in what is publicly taught about the history of white and black people.

7a. *Negative Aspects of European History (EN)*

Europeans throughout history have exhibited various uncivilized behaviors. Over the years they have consistently demonstrated their barbaric nature through unadulterated violence, particularly genocide, suicide and homicide. Cannibalism, incest and molestation of their young were all common cultural practices. But you were never taught these concepts as history education is grotesquely unbalanced. These negative attributes of European history are not promoted in the classroom the way the positive attributes are. In fact, these negative aspects of white history are ignored, hidden or twisted

What You Were Not Taught (The Truth)

into heroic tales of tragedy. Truth be told, the murder, incest and cannibalism are perverted actions of a once uncivilized people. A plethora of examples of the Europeans savagery come directly from the so-called 'Father of History', Herodotus. Herodotus was a European who lived in 5th century B.C. and wrote a history book titled *The Histories*. *The Histories* was Herodotus' interpretation and explanation of various events that occurred during and prior to his life. *The Histories* documents the lives and ways of countless Europeans, their cultures, their interactions with each other and their interactions with other people of the world. Since the man was given the moniker 'the Father of History' (which should really be the Father of European History), the importance, respect and admiration of his work by all historians and society goes without saying. *The Histories* is Herodotus' interpretation and explanation of past events from his perspective as influenced by his environment, education and experiences and it has been studied by millions all around the world for the last 2,400 years. Since its completion in 425 B.C, millions of copies of *The Histories* have been published in scores of languages all over the world. Just over the last 20 years, hundreds of thousands of copies of *The Histories* has been reprinted by at least seven publishers and recorded on tape and CD in several languages. It is studied in university courses all over the world and its massive amount of examples of European barbarity is completely ignored.

One of the most vivid examples of the Europeans' uncivilized, barbaric and genocidal nature is given on pages 48-55 of *The Histories*. A Scynthian[1] king named Astyages had dreams that destruction would come from his daughter's, Mandane, genitals. Once he dreamed that Mandane urinated so much that she flooded his kingdom, all of Europe and all of Asia. After his daughter married Cambyses, Astyages had another dream of a vine growing out of his daughter's genitals that engulfed his entire kingdom. These dreams were interpreted as

75

What You Were Not Taught (The Truth)

a prediction that Mandane's unborn child would usurp Astyages' kingdom from him. Mandane and Cambyses eventually had a son, Cyrus. Due to his dreams, King Astyages immediately ordered the murder of his own grandson Cyrus by a man named Harpagus. Harpagus was a relative of King Astyages and also his most loyal servant.

Now, one would think that a grandfather, Astyages, ordering the murder of his own grandson, Cyrus, by another one of his relatives is as barbaric as it gets. You would think it can't get any more barbaric than a public figure ordering the death of his daughter's newborn child because of a dream, but you ain't read nothing yet. Harpagaus was ordered by Astyages to take baby Cyrus to his home and kill him. Well, Harpagus looking a little into the future when Astyages' daughter Mandane would one day rule, decided it was best that he not kill the child himself. So instead he sent for a herdsman and instructed the herdsman to kill the baby under direct order of Astyages. It just so happened, the herdsman's wife had recently had a baby that was still-born. So instead of killing Astyages grandson, the herdsman was persuaded by his wife to keep baby Cyrus and use the corpse of their dead son as proof that the baby was slain. Needless to say, 10 years later Astayges found out that Harpagus had not murdered Cyrus as ordered. King Astyages did not immediately act with anger. Instead King Astyages explained to Harpagus how his daughter Mandane had resented him for the last 10 years for ordering the execution of her son (his grandson), but now since the boy was still alive he can reconcile with her. He then told Harpagus, hey, send your son over to play with the boy, then you come over later for dinner. To make a long story short, Harpagus sent his thirteen year old son over and King Astyages murdered Harpagus' son, cut him up then cooked his body parts (with the exception of the boy's head, hands and feet). Of course when Harpagus arrived for dinner, guess what he ate? King Astyages fed Harpagus' own son to him for dinner! After Harpagus ate until he was full, Astyages then told him that he just ate his own son and showed him the uncooked head, hands and feet to prove it![2] Why, all because of a dream. THIS IS PURE UNCIVILIZED BARBARISM THAT YOU WERE NOT TAUGHT! First off, the king ordered the death of his own grandson and then punished the man who did not have the heart to kill the infant by killing the man's son and feeding the son to the father. That is barbaric. No matter what type of dramatic spin you try to put on it. If you do not believe these recorded actions of a royal white monarch and his family, then go get the book and read it. It is understandable if you find these facts unbelievable because you have been manipulated by the force (as described in Chapter 2) to believe that savage, barbaric and uncivilized whites never existed, therefore you are driven straight to disbelief. But, ask yourself this question, if these events supposedly happened in Africa, would you have any difficulty accepting them as absolute truth? Most likely, you would not since the force has effectively manipulated you to believe that Africans are inherently savage, barbaric and uncivilized. Just remember, these historical events between Astyages, Harpagus, Mandane, Cambyses and the child Cyrus were interpreted and explained by the worldly respected Herodotus, the 'Father of History'.

The Histories contains countless other documented accounts of white barbarism and incivility. In fact, very crude behavior still exists later down the line in this same family. Cyrus' son Cambyses, who later ruled Persia, murdered his brother Smerdis simply because he had a dream of Smerdis sitting on a throne.[3] THAT IS INSANITY! This same Cambyses also married both of his sisters at a time when "the Persians were on no account accustomed to intermarry with their sisters," which leads one to believe that there was a time when it was customary for Persians to marry their sisters. (This will be discussed in-depth later in this book). To top things off, Cambyses beat his younger wife/sister so viciously that she miscarried their unborn baby and then died.[4] HOW SAVAGE! These are barbarians and by no means were these isolated acts of barbarism, savagery and violence by this one family. Herodotus exposed many culture wide and cross cultural characteristics of European savagery. On page 61 of *The Histories*, Herodotus stated that the Persians are well known for borrowing traits of other cultures and eventually adopting them for their own. Herodotus continues to divulge that "they practice all kinds of indulgences with which they become acquainted; among others, they have learned from the Greeks a passion for boys."[5] PERVERSION THAT YOU WERE NOT TAUGHT! Herodotus describes a savage Issedonian ritual as follows:

> When a man's father dies, all his relations bring cattle, and then, having sacrificed them and cut up the flesh, they cut up also the dead parent of their host, and, having mingled all the flesh together, they spread out a banquet; then, having made bare and cleansed his head [skull], they gild [paint] it; and afterward treat it as a sacred image performing grand annual sacrifices to it.[6]

Are these not the actions of barbarians? If this was an African tradition, it would certainly be considered barbaric. Herodotus reaffirms this practice in another section as follows:

> [W]hen a man has attained a great age, all his kinsmen meet, and sacrifice him, together with cattle of several kinds; and when they have boiled [all] the flesh, they feast on it. This death they account the most happy ; for they do not eat the bodies of those who die of disease, but bury them in the earth, and think it a great misfortune that they did not reach the age to be sacrificed [and eaten].[7]

Herodotus continued to expose the uncivilized nature by explaining how the daughters of every lower class Lydian worked

What You Were Not Taught (The Truth)

as prostitutes, every Babylonian woman is required to have sex with a strange man in some sex temple and the Massagatae men share their wives with one another.[8] Yet another example of their barbarism and unprecedented violence is provided on pages 257-8 of *The Histories* as follows:

> When a Scythian overthrows his first enemy, he drinks his blood; and presents the king with the heads of the enemies he has killed in battle ; for if he brings a head, he shares the booty that they take, but not if he does not bring one. He skins it in the following manner. Having made a circular incision round the ears and taking hold of the skin, he shakes it from the skull ; then, having scraped off the flesh with the rib of an ox, he softens the skin with his hands, and having made it supple, he uses it as a napkin : each man hangs it on the bridle of the horse which he rides, and prides himself on it, for whoever has the greatest number of these skin napkins is accounted the most valiant man. Many of them make cloaks of these skins to throw over themselves, sewing them together like shepherd's coats ; and many, having flayed [skinned] the right hands of their enemies that are dead, together with the nails, make coverings for their quivers: the skin of a man, which is both thick and shining, surpasses almost all other skins in the brightness of its white. Many, having flayed [skinned] men whole, and stretched the skin on wood, carry it about on horseback. Such usages are received among them. 65. The heads themselves, not indeed of all, but of their greatest enemies, they treat as follows : each, having sawn off all below the eye-brows, cleanses it, and if the man is poor, he covers only the outside with leather, and so uses it; but if he is rich, he

> covers it indeed with leather, and, having gilded the inside, he so uses it for a drinking-cup. And they do this to their relatives if they are at variance, and one prevails over [kills] another in the presence of the king. When strangers of consideration come to him, he produces these heads, and relates how, though they were his relatives, they made war against him, and he overcame them, considering this a proof of bravery.[9]

IT SHOULD BE CONSIDERED GENOCIDAL SAVAGERY! Picture two brothers having a disagreement in front of the king, that disagreement leading to a fight to the death and then to one man using his blood brother's freshly scraped skull as a cup. It just does not get any more savage than that. Although wearing a scalp coat and using the skin of a man's right arm with hands and nails still attached as a sheath for a sword are quite savage acts as well. If these were the actions of Africans, they would be labeled 'ignorant savages' without hesitation.

You were not taught of the savage side of Europeans but, I guarantee you were taught of some savage Africans living in the jungle, butt naked, eating their babies. Most of you have probably never even heard of the Scynthians, Issedonians, Lydians or Massagetae. Wonder why? It's because these uncivilized Europeans were erased out of your public education because they exposed the uncivilized nature of whites. Certainly you know of the Persians and the Greeks, but it is not likely you knew about their incest and shared cultural trait of having sex with boys. Certainly you have heard of the Babylonians, but it is not likely you knew about the sanctuary of Aphrodite where each Babylonian woman at some point in her life had to sit and wait for a strange man to come have sex with her. You were only taught one side of the white story, the good side.

The Romans were also a very violent, uncivilized people. No one in the Roman Empire was safe from rampant Italian

What You Were Not Taught (The Truth)

homicide nor the overall violence and savage nature of the Roman people. Even the Roman Emperors were all too often the victim of Roman violence. Of the first 12 Roman Emperors, 2 committed suicide and 6 were viciously assassinated.[10] Miraculously the pure violence and deceit of the Roman people are translated to fairy-tale type stories of love, hate, drama and romance when taught to you in school. In reality, they are exhibitions of barbarism. From Julius Caesar on there is a long trail of blood that parallels the procession of Roman rulers. After battling Mark Anthony, Julius Caesar's adopted son Octavian, who later changed his name to Augustus, took over as Emperor of Rome. You were probably taught that Octavian's claim to fame was promoting high morals throughout the Roman Empire. What you were not taught was that Octavian had numerous affairs and his own daughter Julia hosted orgies on a regular basis right in the Roman Forum. Unfortunately for Octavian, he did not have any sons of his own and made the mistake of declaring his step-son Tiberius heir to his throne. Octavian's declaration was unfortunate because soon after Octavian's wife/Tiberius' mother poisoned Octavian so her son could take over as Emperor sooner rather than later. PURE VICIOUSNESS! Tiberius loved seclusion and spent most of his time on the island of Capri where he feasted on peacock brains and flamingo tongue and entertained himself by having young boys perform sexual acts for him. It is documented that those young boys who refused to get sexually abused had their legs broken. Tiberius continued with his sick behavior, condemning hundreds to death for false charges and he even had a Roman Senator executed for carrying a coin with his face on it into a bathroom. The Roman people under his rule reciprocated his uncivilized ways and Tiberius was eventually smothered to death. Tiberius' adopted grand-son Caligula was the next so called 'mighty Emperor' to rule Rome. Caligula was a pure nut-job teetering on the brink of insanity. Caligula had severe psychological trauma

81

What You Were Not Taught (The Truth)

as his adopted grand-father Tiberius, murdered his mother and two of his brothers. Caligula had Roman citizens chopped up for pet food on a regular basis, made plans to have his horse declared a counsel of Rome and ultimately declared himself a god. The Roman Senate ordered his death and a Roman soldier stabbed him to death. AGAIN, THIS IS PURE INSANITY, BUT I GUARANTEE IT WAS NOT PRESENTED TO YOU IN THIS MANNER. Emperor Claudius was murdered by his wife so her son Nero, Claudius' step son, could become Emperor. Of course, once Nero was emperor what do you think he did? Nero turned right around and murdered his mother! That vicious apple did not fall very far from the tree did it? Nero even outdid his mother as he not only murdered her, but he also murdered his first two wives and had one of his male lovers castrated. By the way, one of his wives was pregnant with their unborn child at the time he murdered her with his own hands. Again, Roman citizens reciprocated the violence of their ruler and the Roman Senate ordered his execution, but Nero stabbed himself in the neck before they could get to him. THESE ARE BEHAVIORS OF AN UNCIVILIZED PEOPLE! Other Roman emperors exercised similar violent actions and homosexual activity in their everyday lives. In fact the Emperor Hadrian, while married, openly flaunted his male private escorts and while in his 50's found 'true love' with a teenage boy named Antinous. See, none of these freakish behaviors of the Roman rulers were divulged to you during your formal education.[11] And these are just the actions of the so-called 'prestigious' royal Roman Emperors. Now, with that level of barbarity regularly exhibited at the top of the Roman hierarchy, one could only imagine what was going on at the so-called 'bottom' of Roman Empire. One example which says it all was the boisterous cheering of Roman citizens in the infamous Roman Coliseum as their fellow human beings were devoured by wild animals. That was pure barbarism and should be

82

honestly presented as such and not spin-doctored into some honorable battle between man and beast.

The Persian Emperor Constantine was another murderous killer portrayed as a great European Emperor. Many historians refer to him as 'Constantine the Great', the 'First Christian Emperor of the Roman World'. In fact Constantine, who was a gargantuan proponent and promoter of Christianity, was at some point in time designated as a saint, St. Constantine. Well, besides being the 'Great Saint', Constantine was a ruthless, savage killer who without hesitation murdered immediate family members and non-family members alike. Constantine murdered two wives (one of which he had been married to for twenty years and had seven children with), one of his sons, two brothers-in-law, a father-in-law and three nephews. His sister, the mother of one of the murdered nephews and wife of one of the murdered brothers-in-law, eventually went mad and committed suicide since her brother killed her husband and her son. This short list only includes the family members that Constantine murdered. There are many non-family members who were slain by the sword of the savage Saint Constantine. He killed many of his father's friends and trusted allies not long after taking over the throne and killed his son's friends the same time he slaughtered his son Crispus. Constantine openly threatened and murdered any who did not accept and practice Christianity and once had an infant slayed just so its insides could be observed.[12] Constantine was a dysfunctional serial killer, but yet today's historians, who should know about all of these vile acts of barbarism, still refer to Constantine as 'Great' and a 'Saint' in the classroom. All of Constantine's savage murders are conveniently ignored in the history curriculum as European history is predominantly portrayed from a positive angle. When you heard Constantine's story, the focus was on how he expanded his kingdom and on his theoretical love of Christianity, not the uncontested fact that he killed his family and many other innocent Europeans. His uncivilized, barbaric, and down right nasty nature may have been mentioned, but by no means were they the focus of your teachers' Constantine lesson plans.

Even the history lessons of Europeans commonly referred to as barbarians, the Vikings, the Goths, the Vandals and the Huns, were manipulative. Serious word-play in describing these northern European barbarians attempted to mask the truth. One history program referred to these murderous brutes as "God's Appointees for War" whose killing, robbing and raping sprees were "divinely ordained so these well trained, well equipped warriors adorned with symbols can seize to bring favor of the gods". The program continued to "praise the Vikings' warrior spirit" and reaffirm that they "looked smart decorated with badges of high rank". THIS IS ALL BULL! They were vicious, uncivilized, unsanitary murderers, rapists and thieves. Unbelievably the program continued to describe these people as a "thirsty for glory people who were dedicated to conquest and whose warrior spirit allowed them to conquer and spread their sphere of influence but whose genius was unfortunately sacrificed by their ambition". Translation: they were effective killers who were too busy invading, pillaging, raping and murdering to advance their culture.

All of these FACTS represent 'What You Were Not Taught' about the negative side of European history. Now, armed with a small piece of 'What You Were Not Taught', let's take a minute to revisit Figure 14 of the previous chapter. Before learning of the more savage side of the European, the further categorization of what my classmates and I were taught was severely unbalanced.

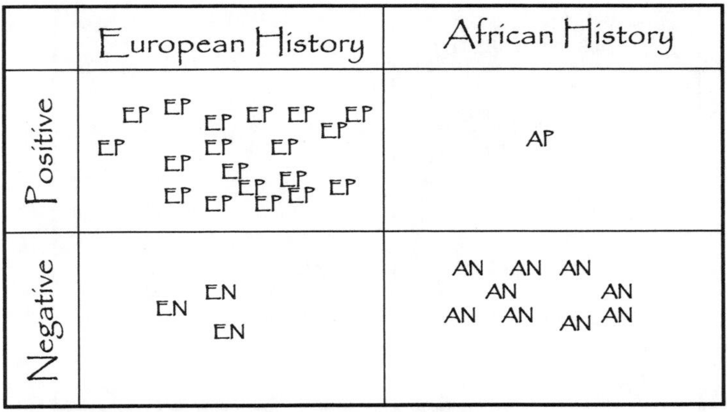

What You Were Not Taught (The Truth)

	European History	African History
Positive	EP EP EP EP EP EP EP EP EP EP EP EP EP EP EP EP EP EP	AP
Negative	EN EN EN EN	AN AN AN AN AN AN AN AN AN

Figure 21 Further categorization of what we were taught.

Our history education disproportionately focused on the positive aspects of Europeans (EP) and negative aspects of Africans and people of African descent (AN). Almost no attention was given to negative aspects of Europeans (EN) nor positive aspects of Africans (AP). But after learning of the savagery of the European (EN) as presented in the previous pages, the balancing process began. Your skewed perspective that Europeans and European descendants are perfect beings who spread tranquility and civilization throughout the world is corrected. Learning of the savagery and barbarism of the European helps to balance your education of the people of the world. Figure 22 reflects the balancing effect of the previous pages on your knowledge base. Notice how the EN quadrant (bottom, left) which depicts the amount of historical facts that portray Europeans in a negative light is now in balance with the AN quadrant (bottom, right) which depicts the amount of historical facts that portray Africans in a negative light.

85

What You Were Not Taught (The Truth)

	European History	African History
Positive	EP EP EP EP EP EP EP EP EP EP EP EP EP EP EP EP EP EP	AP
Negative	EN EN EN EN EN EN EN EN EN	AN AN AN AN AN AN AN AN AN

Figure 22 Partial balancing of our education with the previously mentioned EN's added.

After mapping the documented savagery on to the chart, some semblance of balance is now achieved. Learning of these negative historical occurrences of the European neutralizes the undeserving aura of superiority created by learning of only the positive accomplishments of white people. This neutralization is accomplished by balancing the amount of positive European historical facts (EP) with the negative (EN).

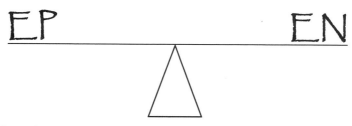

Figure 23 Notice the balance created by learning positive as well as negative aspects of European history.

You now realize that Europeans and their descendants are not superior to any other people of the world. You realize that they are humans who have done good and bad. You realize that Europeans and their descendants are the same as other races of people in the world, they have a positive side (EP) the school system made sure you learned and they have a negative side (EN) you have just read in the preceding pages. You now know that like Africans and African descendants, Europeans have a very negative side of history.

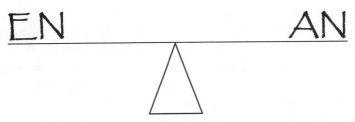

Figure 24 Notice the balance created by learning negative aspects of both European history and African history.

The addition of some negative aspects of European history helps to complete the full matrix of truth. Each letter of each word counts as a weight in helping to balance your education. If you take another look at the chart, you will notice that one quadrant is still scarcely populated. The top right quadrant, which represents positive historical facts of Africans and African descendants, needs grave attention in order to complete the balancing. The last type of weight necessary to fully balance your education is the rich, positive aspect of African history covered next.

7b. *Positive Aspects of African History (AP)*

As stated earlier, there is great magnificence, pride and superiority that surround Africans and African descendants exemplified by cultured, educated and sophisticated acts of African pharaohs, kings, queens, priests, warriors, educators and citizens. Logic demands that Africans would be the first to reach civilization and prosperity since they were the first humans on earth. To date, the oldest remains of humans found by Drs. Louis S. B. and Mary Leaky and other subsequent archeologists have been in Eastern **AFRICA;** and since 1959, there have been numerous other archaeological finds to prove that Africa is the birth place of man. No archaeological digs in any other part of the world, including Europe, has come up with remains older than those found in Africa. The profession of anthropology has been in existence for hundreds of years yet European anthropologists and archaeologists did not find any significant fossil discoveries in relation to human origin until 1959. The tardy discovery was due to the influence of the force. European archeologists never looked to Africa as the source of humankind as they were convinced by the force that Africa was full of uncivilized savages who under no circumstances could be the source of human origin. These European archaeologists searched Europe high and low for physical justification they created civilization. It was never found in Europe. Dr. Leakey, born to European missionaries in Africa, finally took the search to Africa. Truth be told, the world knew Africa was the birthplace of civilization way before 1959 and prior to any of these archeological discoveries. Back in the 5th century B.C. the same Herodotus, European proclaimed 'Father of History' told the world the fact that Africans were the first men on earth when he wrote "Where the meridian declines toward the setting sun, the Ethiopian territory reaches, being the extreme part of the habitable world. It produces much gold, huge elephants, wild trees of all kind, ebony, and men of large stature, very handsome, and long-lived".[13] Again, *The Histories* is Herodotus' interpretation and explanation of past events from his perspective as influenced by his environment, education and experiences and it has been studied by millions all around the world for the last 2,400 years. Since its completion in 425 B.C, millions of copies of *The Histories* has been issued in scores of languages all over the world. Just over last 20 years, hundreds of thousands of copies of *The Histories* has been reprinted by at least seven publishers and recorded on tape and CD in several languages. It is studied in universities all over the world yet Herodotus' numerous compliments to Africans for their achievements of humanity are somehow conveniently overlooked and ignored. Herodotus reaffirms the African origin of civilization in several other sections of *The Histories*. On page 100 he states, "For my own part, I am not of opinion that the Egyptians commenced their existence with the country which the Ionians call Delta, but that they always were since men have been."[14] **AFRICANS WERE THE FIRST MEN ON EARTH AND ARE THE FATHERS OF CIVILIZATION!!** This fact must be explicitly stated to negate the false beliefs that Europeans brought civilization to Africa. Professor Diop in describing various Egyptian wall paintings points out that "all the specimens of the White race were placed behind the Blacks; in particular, the "blond beast" of Gobineau and the Nazis, a tattooed savage, dressed in animal skin, instead of being at the start of all civilization, was still essentially untouched by it and occupied the last echelon of humanity."[15] These ancient Africans developed writing, commerce, government, law, the calendar, etc. and left the hieroglyphic evidence on pyramid and temple walls as proof. Ancient Africans in Egypt, Africa laid the basic characteristics of human civilization that are still used to this day. These black men, women and children of the Nile Valley were chosen by God to define humanity for us all and they did so thousands of years before any foreign influence.

Dr. Indus Khamit-Kush in his masterpiece *What They Never Told You In History Class* quotes Auguste Mariette from his work *Outlines of Ancient Egyptian History*:

> "While as yet the world in general was plunged
> in the depths of barbarism; and the nations that

later on were to play so important a part in the
world's history were still savages, the banks of
the Nile were nurturing a people both cultivated
and civilized; and a powerful monarchy, aided by
a complete organization of court functionaries
and civil servants, was already ruling the fate of
the nation. However far into the dim past we
gaze, we are everywhere met by a fully
developed civilization to which the succeeding
centuries, numerous as they are, have added
nothing."[16]

The pre-dynastic kings and plethora of dynastic pharaohs were
the architects of civilization and they were Africans. They had
black skin, full lips, wide noses and ruled thousands of years
before Europeans were around.

Civilization as we know it was originally developed under
the authority of the pre-dynastic and post-dynastic African kings,
queens and pharaohs, but yet somehow you were not taught
anything about them. Again, Herodotus states that Egyptians
"always were since men have been."[17] These African men and
women should be universally recognized heroes of the world, but
instead they are basically ignored in the classroom. These
magnificent Africans had the vision as well as the social,
financial and technological resources to build massive pyramids
up to the sky, and they did. The monstrous pyramids remain to
this day as evidence of the power of the Nile Valley Africans, but
yet for some reason the education system does not feel
obligated to recognize these great ancient Africans and teach
you about them. Instead your educators' flawed perspective as
perpetuated by the force lead them straight to disbelief and
consequently the credit for building such perfect, complex,
astronomically relevant mega structures which rightfully
belonged to the Africans was given to some aliens or Martians.
There are volumes of books and numerous websites that support

the concept of aliens building the pyramids. You inherited this backward philosophy and were subliminally discouraged not to take the time to search out the full truth. Your teachers may have well flat out stated 'aliens must have built the pyramids because niggers are not smart enough and are too lazy to build something like that', as that idea emanates when the Africans' credit for building the pyramids was given to aliens. Be notified that society as it exists today **WOULD NOT BE** without these great black rulers, but somehow their enormous contributions are ignored in history class. These great Africans laid the groundwork for modern civilization. They established the model of government, developed medicine and created the basis of modern religion, but you were not taught anything about them. Here is a challenge*: With the exception of King Tut can you list 5 pharaohs and identify what they are best known for?* Can you? Better yet, if you were given a list of 5 pharaohs and a list of 5 characteristics, would you be able to match each pharaoh with their respective characteristic? Are you able to simply name one African pharaoh you learned of in school? Can you name the pharaoh pictured on the cover of this book? Here is a list; you are challenged to a match game. On the diagram below, please match each pharaoh with what he is best known for:

African Pharaoh	Best Known As
King Tutankahmon	The Monotheistic Pharaoh
Pharaoh Djoser	The first Pharaoh of the 1st Dynasty
Pharaoh Rameses II	The Boy King
Pharaoh Akhenaten	The Pyramid Builder
Pharaoh Narmer	The most powerful Pharaoh who ever lived

Could you do it? If so, excellent! If not, do not feel ashamed as the opportunity to add knowledge is about to present itself.

What You Were Not Taught (The Truth)

The Old Kingdom

As stated earlier, Pharaoh Aha also known as Pharaoh Menses and Pharaoh Narmer was the very first formal pharaoh of the very first formal Egyptian Dynasty. There were numerous other kings who ruled Upper and Lower Egypt during its pre-dynastic history, but King Narmer united all the Southern city-states into one. Next he united the Northern Kingdom with his Southern Kingdom thusly starting the first formal Dynasty of Egyptian history. In fact, Professor John G. Jackson certifies that sixty kings ruled in one particular area of Lower Egypt before Pharaoh Narmer unified the North and the South.[18] The foundation of civilization was developed under these pre-dynastic vassal kings during the pre-dynastic period while the more complex aspects of civilization and the expansion of the Egyptian Kingdom occurred during the post-dynastic period beginning with Pharaoh Narmer. After unification, Pharaoh Narmer directed the building of a metropolis at Memphis, Egypt to serve as the capital of his new kingdom. In order to use the specific location he chose as the headquarters for his kingdom, a dam had to be built to redirect the flow of the Nile, a monstrous task on its own. Narmer had the dam constructed and successfully established his capital at Memphis, Egypt. Here is a bust of the majestic pioneer King Narmer:

Figure 25 Bust of Pharaoh Narmer.

92

What You Were Not Taught (The Truth)

Again, the very basis of civilization was developed by the pre-dynastic kings of the Nile Valley while more complex aspects of civilization were developed under the pharaohs. And Pharaoh Narmer's immediate successors did just that. Pharaohs Djoser, Snefru, Khufu, Khafre and Menkaure who ruled during the IIIrd and IVth Dynasties continued to propagate more complicated aspects of civilization by creating the concept of and building astronomically pertinent super structures, the Pyramids. Immense human and financial resources had to be effectively managed to build the great pyramids. Plans had to be drawn; resources had to be coordinated; stones had to be mined; laborers had to be fed and clothed; doctors had to be available to treat injuries and sickness; tools had to be provided; and most importantly an environment of prosperity had to be maintained by the pharaohs to allow their people to erect Pyramids in the pharaohs' name. In just about every case, not only were these pharaohs highly respected for the joyous civilization they shouldered but they were considered living gods. Each structure required millions of stones, thousands of supporters and a number of years to erect and the pharaohs provided the peaceful and wealthy kingdoms necessary to facilitate the Pyramid building process. Keep in mind, all the stones had to be mined, laborers required food, clothing, shelter, tools, health care, etc. for an extensive amount of time. Each of these great pharaohs afforded all the resources necessary for years on in for the sake of leaving massive symbols of their massive legacies, which still stand 4,500 years later. Pharaoh Djoser following the engineering foundation laid by King Narmer started the African pyramid building phenomenon when he had his African architect Imhotep engineer the 204 foot Step Pyramid at Saqqara. While it was Djoser who provided the environment and resources and came to be known as the Pyramid Builder, it was Imhotep who engineered the Step Pyramid along with many other buildings in the city of Saqqara. In addition to being a ground-breaking

93

architect, Imhotep was a well respected philosopher, astronomer and prized physician. In fact, he is often referred to as the proper 'God of Medicine'. Here is a statue of Pharaoh Djoser and a photo of the Step Pyramid at Saqqara and the Saqqara Temple erected by Djoser and Imhotep.

Figure 26 Statue of Pharaoh Djoser.

Figure 27 Pharaoh Djoser's Step Pyramid engineered by Imhotep.

What You Were Not Taught (The Truth)

Figure 28 Pharaoh Djoser's Saqqara Temple engineered by Imhotep.

The next set of Pyramids, the Bent Pyramid and the Red Pyramid, were erected by Pharaoh Snefru during the IVth Dynasty at Dahshur. In conjunction with the African culture and in the spirit of positive forward progress, Snefru built not one, but two pyramids, the tallest to an unprecedented 340 feet which is 132 feet taller than Pharaoh Djoser's Step Pyramid. Here are photos of Snefru's Bent and Red Pyramids.

Figure 29 Snefru's Bent Pyramid.

95

What You Were Not Taught (The Truth)

Figure 30 Snefru's Red Pyramid.

Pharaoh Khufu, Pharaoh Snefru's son, was next in line and built the most massive Pyramid of them all. Khufu erected the massive Great Pyramid at Giza. Khufu's Pyramid stands 482 feet high and its base takes up 13 acres of land. Pharaoh Khufu's Great Pyramid is one of the 'Seven Wonders of the World' and the most prominent engineers of the last 4,500 years continuously marvel at its construction. Here is a statue of Pharaoh Khufu and a photo of his Great Pyramid:

Figure 31 Statue of Pharaoh Khufu (enlarged photo included to highlight the pharaoh's unmistakable African facial features).

What You Were Not Taught (The Truth)

Figure 32 Pharaoh Khufu's Great Pyramid.

Archaeologist digging at Giza happened to come across one of Khufu's buried boats. Khufu's Solar Barge as it is known is 141 feet long and approximately 4,600 years old. Now, in 1492 (A.D.) Columbus sailed the ocean blue, but Pharaoh Khufu and other ancient Africans were sailing around 2600 B.C., some 4,100 years before Columbus was born. Now, you were taught that 1) Columbus discovered America and 2) before he set out to sea, people thought the world was flat. If Africans were sailing 4,100 years before Columbus was born, is it not logical that they would have ventured out past the Nile River, into the Mediterranean Sea and further onto the Atlantic, Indian and Pacific Oceans some years before 1492? Is it not logical to conclude that ancient Africans sometime within their 4,100 years of experience on the water sailed out past the horizon and noted that the world was not flat? Why it is extremely logical. Ancient Egyptian priests and astronomers already knew the world was round but you were not taught anything about them, Pharaoh Khufu or his Solar Barge. So when your teachers told you Columbus discovered America and 'people' thought the world was flat, what they really meant

97

was Columbus was the first European to make it close to America and 'European people' thought the world was flat because they taught you from the dominant European perspective. No consideration was given to ancient Africans and their seafaring expeditions during your World History course despite the fact that Khufu's Solar Barge is currently housed in an African museum.

Figure 33 Pharaoh Khufu's Solar Barge.

Ancient Africans were sailing even prior to Khufu's time. It is illogical for one to believe Europeans were able to overcome the Africans 4,000 year head-start on nautical experience and reach the shores of North America before ancient Africans; and it was down right disrespectful for the curriculum to direct your third grade teacher to teach you such a concept. Even worse, your teacher did not tell you about all the ancient African artifacts and European sailors' documentation which serves as evidence Africans reached North and South America years before Europeans. The most prominent evidence being African stone statues left in Mexico and surrounding areas. The most

98

prominent series of these artifacts are the massive Olmec stone heads. One is pictured below:

Figure 34 An example of one of the massive Olmec stone heads found in Mexico. Notice the undeniable African features!

Pharaoh Khafre, Pharaoh Khufu's son, like his father built the second massive Pyramid at Giza. Unlike his father who built the Great Pyramid at Giza, Khafre was not able to erect a structure larger than his predecessors. But to make up for it, Khafre had another structure erected in his likeness, the Great Sphinx. Pharaoh Khafre's pyramid is 447 feet high. Pharaoh Khafre was able to provide the same prosperity necessary to allow the construction of the massive structure along with food, clothing, shelter, medical care and a certain level of morale to keep his followers happy. His followers also built the Great Sphinx for Pharaoh Khafre at the same site. Before its face was blown off by Napoleon's troops it exhibited the same African facial characteristics as Pharaoh Khafre's statue below. The Sphinx has been a long standing symbol of Egypt, Africa and it was erected by Africans for their divine Pharaoh Khafre. Here is

What You Were Not Taught (The Truth)

a statue of Pharaoh Khafre, and a photo of his Sphinx with his pyramid in the background:

Figure 35 Statue of Pharaoh Khafre.

Figure 36 Pharaoh's Khafre's Great Sphinx with his Pyramid in the background.

What You Were Not Taught (The Truth)

The third pyramid at Giza was erected by Pharaoh Khafre's son, Pharaoh Menkaure. Here is a statue of Pharaoh Menkaure and a photo of his pyramid.

Figure 37 Pharaoh Menkaure.

Figure 38 Menkaure's Pyramid.

What You Were Not Taught (The Truth)

While erecting the Pyramids was a huge accomplishment, Old Kingdom pharaohs did even more to develop human civilization. Miles of hieroglyphic texts and wall paintings were etched in stone and written on papyrus (paper) to document the first human history, philosophic thought, medical procedures, prayers and literature. Much of the papyrus documentation has not survived time, but the stone obelisks and tomb writings have. Tomb walls contain countless writings documenting the political and social accomplishments of their eternal inhabitants and stating specific prayers for their journey to the afterlife. The Old Kingdom pharaohs defined what a pharaoh should be and the world should be grateful for what they did for the human race. Unfortunately, all good things must come to an end and after an extensive and very prosperous rule of Pepi II many regional rulers were able to gain enough power to cause political disturbances throughout the land. After about 1,000 years of prosperity, the Egypt, Africa government was decentralized after Pepi's death for a short period.

What You Were Not Taught (The Truth)

The Middle Kingdom

After a brief Intermediate Period, Egypt, Africa was again united under the powerful Pharaoh Mentuhotep I:

Figure 39 Statue of Pharaoh Mentuhotep I.

Mentuhotep I ruled for 50 years and was able to re-establish the traditional environment of peace and prosperity for his people. Mentuhotep I kicked off another long and prosperous period for ancient Africans. Another pharaoh who ruled during the Middle Kingdom was Amenemhet I. Amenemhet I enacted religious and political changes in the kingdom to benefit his people and protected Egypt's borders', particularly its north-eastern border from the Asiatics. Amenemhet's I son, Senusret I defined his

What You Were Not Taught (The Truth)

own legacy by advancing his father's. Instead of simply protecting Egypt's borders, Senusret I advanced the Egyptian border. Senusret I advanced the Egyptian army further north out of Africa and conquered lands in India and Southern Europe. A few generations down the line, Amenemhet III ruled the Egyptian, African Kingdom. Amenemhet III bought immense economic growth to Egypt, mostly from his mining and quarrying expeditions in Africa and the Sinai penninsula. Hieroglyphic inscriptions still remain in turquoise mines in Sinai that document his expeditions. Here is a statue of Pharaoh Amenemhet III:

Figure 40 Statue of Pharaoh Amenemhet III.

Pure Africans and pure Africans alone ruled the first 14 Dynasties of Egypt, Africa history. From Zinjanthrous Boise up to the 15th Dynasty, Africans developed and advanced human civilization without influence of any Europeans. Humanity as we know it today was developed under the formal authority of indigenous Africans of Egypt. Pharaohs had successfully

What You Were Not Taught (The Truth)

defended their borders against white barbarians from the north for years on in, but finally during the 15th Dynasty the Hyksos were able to temporarily capture the northern piece of the African Kingdom. The Hyksos domination of northern Egypt represented yet another split of Egypt and regenerated separate Northern and Southern Kingdoms. The foreign Hyksos rule of northern Egypt infuriated the proud Africans of the south and they soon took action to regain the northern part of their territory. A great African warrior king would emerge from the south to reclaim the Northern Kingdom for indigenous Africans. Pharaoh Kamose took his army and invaded the Hyksos capital in Avaris. Unfortunately Kamose was not successful in his march and was killed in battle. In Kamose's honor, his younger brother Ahmose I took up the cause of expelling the Hyksos out of Africa. Ahmose I at the young age of 20, took his army into Avaris, defeated the Hyksos and expelled them out of Africa. The battles of both Kamose and Ahmose I are documented, in stone. Kamose's documentation is the Carnarvon Tablet which for some reason is in the British Museum and Ahmose's battles are documented in one of his soldier's tombs at Nekheb. Pharaoh Ahmose's I defeat and expulsion of the Hyksos out of Egypt marks the beginning of the New Kingdom.

The New Kingdom

Pharaoh Ahmose I and the New Kingdom returned stability to the Egyptian Kingdom. Africans during the New Kingdom experienced their most wide spread domination of foreign peoples. The first woman pharaoh, Queen Hatshepsut inherited a peaceful kingdom and did not see the need to attack others. Instead the queen erected temples and tombs and used the army to begin trading with her fellow Africans in the land of Phunt. As the first woman pharaoh, she put forth much effort to ensure her followers respect. Judging from the magnificent

105

statues and temples they erected for her, Hatshepsut was successful. Pharaoh Hatshepsut's successor was Pharaoh Tuthmosis III. Pharaoh Tuthmosis' focus was not only defending but expanding the Egyptian Kingdom. Pharaoh Tuthmosis III launched numerous attacks on several western Asia states, all of which were successful. He had a scribe named Thanuny document every battle and every victory on the walls of the temple of Karnak. Tuthmosis made it a point to attack Syria every summer for eighteen years straight and it is documented on the walls at Karnak that Tuthmosis III conquered over 350 cities during his reign, but you were not taught anything about him. Sadly, an obliesk completed by Tuthmosis IV which includes details of Tuthmosis' III battles stands in front of St. John Lateran in Rome after it was stolen out of Africa.

Due to the military prowess of Pharaoh Tuthmosis III, his great-grandson Pharaoh Amenhotep III did not need much military activity. His reign was extremely prosperous and the stability of his kingdom allowed for the artistic and intellectual development of his people. Here is a statue of Pharaoh Amenhotep III:

Figure 41 Statue of Pharaoh Amenhotep III.

What You Were Not Taught (The Truth)

Pharaoh Amenhotep III passed on a very prosperous, intellectually and artistically live Egyptian Kingdom to his son Amenhotep IV, better known as Pharaoh Akhenaten. Since all of his peoples needs were satisfied, Pharaoh Akhenaten had the leisure to concentrate on desires and his primary desire was monotheism. Akhenaten was one of the first people in history to direct his people toward the concept of one God whom he called Aten. He wrote magnificent religious passages including the Hymn to the Aten which still remains on the tomb of Akhenaten's chief minister, Ay. Pharaoh Akhenaten's religious beliefs made him a very pious ruler and uninterested in military activity. The dutiful pharaoh therefore spent his days with his wife, the famous Queen Nefertiti, promoting monotheistic religion. Here is a statue of Pharaoh Akhenaten:

Figure 42 Statue of the pious Pharaoh Akhenaten (his wife was the more renowned Queen Nefertiti).

The famous boy King Tutankhamun also known as King Tut was married to one of Pharaoh Akhenaten's daughters. He is possibly the most popular of all the Egyptian pharaoh's because of the rich pieces that were taken out of his tomb and put on display by Britain's archaeologist Howard Carter. The most publicized of all these pieces were Tut's golden funerary mask. But other statue's that clearly exemplify his blackness (as depicted on the cover of this text) are not widely shown. Here is another one of Tut's statues from his tomb that exhibit his blackness but is rarely displayed:

Figure 43 Statue of King Tut.

Another very popular pharaoh who you were not taught about is Pharaoh Rameses II also known as Rameses the Great. Rameses the Great possessed exceptional military power and exercised it regularly on his enemies. He did battle with the Syrians and the Hittites and commonly used war captives as slaves to build his grand monuments. The concept of white slaves building monuments for an African pharaoh was never taught to you, but it happened. Your teacher did not have an issue teaching you about the black slaves who harvested cotton for whites, but did not dare mention white slaves who built monuments for blacks. Here is a statue of Rameses the Great, known as the greatest pharaoh who ever lived:

What You Were Not Taught (The Truth)

Figure 44 Statue of Pharaoh Rameses II also known as Rameses the Great.

Rameses III was another African pharaoh who was known to enslave the white people he conquered. Rameses III conquered Europeans in Greece, Assyria, Palestine and Phoenicia and enslaved those whites as he conquered them. He brought many back to Egypt, branded them with a royal Egyptian seal and put them to work while others he enslaved on their former land. Rameses' III life, contributions to Egyptian society, conquers, etc. is documented in hieroglyphic writing on the Great Harris Papyrus, but yet you were taught nothing about him.

Certainly you were taught about the Europeans who were finally able to conquer and cause the downfall of the Egyptian Empire. You were undoubtedly taught about Cambyses, Alexander and Caesar who destroyed Egypt, Africa, but not about Narmer, Djoser, Khufu, Khafre, Menkaure, Pepi I, Pepi II, Mentuhotep I, Metuhotep II, Amenemhet I, Senusret I, Amenemhet II, Senusret II, Senusret III, Amenemhet III,

109

What You Were Not Taught (The Truth)

Kamose, Ahmose I, Amenhotep I, Queen Hatshepsut, Amenhotep II, Amenhotep III, Amenhotep IV(Akhenaten), Tutankhamun, Rameses I, Rameses II(the Great), Rameses III or the hundred other African pharaohs who built it and left hard core evidence as documentation. You were only taught a part of the story, the part that makes Europeans seem almighty and Africans seem savage. You were taught that Cambyses, Alexander and Caesar conquered Egypt, but you were not taught about the ancient knowledge Europeans forced out of the conquered Egyptians. Professor George G. M. James in his masterpiece *Stolen Legacy* states, "[t]he Greeks did not carry culture and learning to Egypt [Africa], but found it already there, and wisely settled in that country, in order to absorb as much as possible of its culture."[19] Indus Khamit-Kush in *What They Never Told You In History Class* quotes several modern and ancient sources that document the European theft of Africans knowledge and claiming it as their own. On page 187 Khamit-Kush quotes Albert Slosman who quoted Clement of Alexandria in *The Book of Life and Beyond* (1919) as follows:

> For let us not forget that it was because of the rampant use of plagiarism among the Greeks, that Clement of Alexandria said at the time: 'A one thousand page book will not be long enough to cite the names of my fellow country-men who have used and abused the Egyptian science.'[20]

On page 157 he quotes S.R.K. Granville editor of *The Legacy of Egypt* (1942) as follows:

> Greek authors point to Egypt as the source of their philosophy. Thales, Solon, Pythagoras, Democritus of Abdera, and Plato are all asserted to have visited Egypt and to have sat at the feet of Egyptian priests . . . Of Pythagoras it is even related that he had been initiated into ancient Egyptian literature by the high priest Sonchis.[21]

What You Were Not Taught (The Truth)

On page 189 Khamit-Kush quotes the ancient Diodorus Siculus when he stated:

> And Lycurgos also, as well as Solon and Plato, are reported to have inserted many of the Egyptian customs into their own codes of laws, while Pythagoras, they say, learned from the Egyptians, the doctrine of divine wisdom, the theorems of geometry, the theory of numbers, and in addition, the transmigration of the soul into every living being.[22]

So when your math teachers taught you the Pythagorean Theorem is $a^2 + b^2 = c^2$, they did not tell you that Pythagoras most likely learned that from African priests and claimed it as his own. You were not taught about the Egyptian doctors who were forced to heal the Europeans' wounds.[23] You did not learn that the Egyptians were the first to discover a birth control recipe and document it on the Ebers Papyrus which the Europeans permanently borrowed as it currently resides in London.[24] Even though the European 'Father of History' Herodotus stated "Egyptians were also the first who introduced public festivals, processions, and solemn supplications ; and the Greeks learned them from them ; for these rites appear to have been established for a very long time, but those in Greece have been lately introduced" you were not taught such a concept.[25] Even though Herodotus also stated the following on page 95 of *The Histories,* you were never taught it:

> [T]he Egyptians were the first to discover the year, which they divided into twelve parts ; and they say that they made this discovery from the stars ; and so far, I think, they act more wisely than the Grecians [Greeks], in that the Grecians insert an intercalary month every third year, on account of the seasons ; whereas the Egyptians, reckoning twelve months of thirty days each,

add five days each year above that number, and
so with them the circle of the seasons comes
round to the same point . . . and most of these
things they proved were so in fact.[26]

You were never taught about the Africans who were able to gain
high positions in European governments even though scores of
them lived very public lives that were documented by past
historians. You were never taught about the African Emperor of
Rome, Septimus Servus; nor of Clitus Niger who served as
cavalry leader for Alexander the Great; nor of Queen Zenobia
the warrior ruler of Palmyra; nor of Johannes Morus (John the
Moor) who was a vizier in Sicily around 1100 A.D. You were
never taught the concept of a Black Madonna (Virgin Mary and
baby Jesus) despite the scores of statues and painting that exist
all over Europe today. In fact, here is one painting of the Black
Madonna that resides in Czestochowa, Poland:

Figure 45 Painting of the Black Madonna.

112

What You Were Not Taught (The Truth)

You were not taught about the three African Popes -- Pope Victor, Pope Miltiades and Pope Gelasius -- or any other religious leader of African descent such as St. Augustine, St. Maurice, Tertullian and Cuprian. In fact, here is a painting of St. Maurice that has been in existence for 480 years:

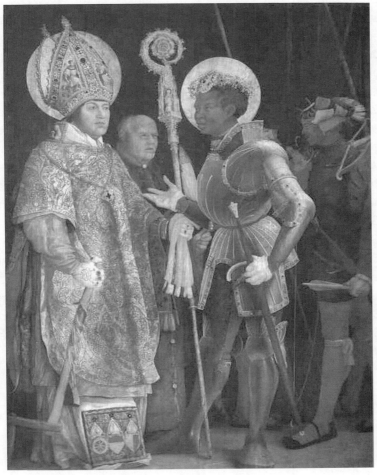

Figure 46 Painting of St. Maurice meeting St. Erasmus by a German named Matthias Grunewald, 1524 A.D.

What You Were Not Taught (The Truth)

You were not taught about the extremely rich kingdoms of Western Africa. You were not taught about the massive Kingdom of Mali founded by the Mandingoes nor of its line of kings, Sundiata, Mansa Wali, nor Mansa Musa I. You were not taught about the Kingdom of Songhay nor of its Kings Sunni Ali the Great, Askia Mohammed I, King Daoud nor of its illustrious Universities in Gao, Jenne and Timbuktu. John G. Jackson specifically identifies that courses in, "astronomy, mathematics, ethnography, medicine, hygiene, philosophy, logic, prosody, diction, elocution, rhetoric, and music" were taught at these pioneering African institutions of higher learning.[27] You were not taught about the great African Generals who attacked southern Europe. You were not taught about General Hannibal Barca who with tens of thousands African warriors and war elephants attacked the Roman Empire during the Punic War. You were not taught about the African General Gibral Tarikh and his conquests in Spain and Portugal; nor of the fact that the Rock of Gibraltar is named after him.[28] You were not taught about the African General Ganges who attacked India; nor of the fact that the Ganges River is named after him.[29] You learned how the Europeans used guns to conquer Africans but not how the Zulu and Ashanti warriors fought the British for hundreds of years resisting their advances. You did not learn about the Zulu King Cetewayo who orchestrated decisive victories over the British in South Africa, killed Prince Napoleon, and held audience with the queen and prime minister of England.[30]

What You Were Not Taught (The Truth)

Figure 47 King Cetewayo, Shaka Zulu's nephew, who held impressive victories over England's imperialistic forces.

You did not learn about the Ethiopian Emperor Menelik II who in 1896 successfully battled Italy to maintain Ethiopian independence. You did not learn about Jomo Kenyatta, Dedan Kamathi and the Mau Mau battles against the British for independence; nor of the Algerian War of Independence from France; nor of the Mozambique, Angola, Guinea-Bissau wars of independence with the Portuguese; nor of the series of Pan African Congresses where prominent African and African American leaders such as W.E.B. DuBois and H. Sylvester Williams gathered in several world capitals such as London, Manchester, New York, Paris and Brussels to generate and execute political demands to end European imperialism in Africa. See, without hesitation you were told of the Europeans conquer and imperialism over the African but not of the African's physical and political battles for independence. The Mau Mau Revolution

What You Were Not Taught (The Truth)

in Kenya against the British lasted for eight years. These Africans were passionate in their battle for independence and pursued their cause by any means. Their goal was to rid their country of their oppressor and they would not stop fighting until that goal was reached. Now, if you were taught anything at all about the Mau Mau, which most likely you were not, there were probably references to these brothers as ruthless terrorist rebels, fanatics or some other negative connotation. Understand, the goal of the Mau Mau was to attain independence for their country from an oppressor. This was the exact same goal as George Washington, but you will never hear any reference to Washington as a ruthless terrorist rebel etc. In fact, the Mau Mau and George Washington even had the exact same oppressor, England, but again you will never hear Washington described with the same negative descriptors as the Mau Mau.

After all the African nations attained their independence they went on to re-establish their own governments. Starting with President Kwame Nkrumah in Ghana, these African nations began to organize and rebuild after years of exploitation by foreign oppressors. Africans used their natural resources to rebuild wealth and re-establish traditional African social and political structures. An essential element to the success of any nation is its economic stability and since the African continent has vast natural resources the rebuilding nations were easily able to establish themselves financially. After reestablishing their government many of the African countries revamped their financial structure, built new national reserves and printed their own currency with pictures of their own indigenous leaders emblazoned upon them. You have been mentally conditioned by images on the television to believe the whole African continent is a third world mess, therefore you may find the following images of African bank notes difficult to comprehend:

116

What You Were Not Taught (The Truth)

What You Were Not Taught (The Truth)

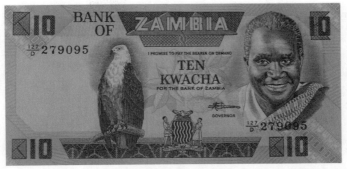

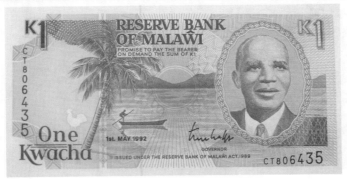

Figure 48 Bank notes of African countries with pictures of their indigenous African leaders forever stamped upon them, none of which you were taught anything about.

Figure 49 Back of bank notes of various African countries.

Figure 50 Back of Kenyan banknote that depicts an African University, African students and African professors.

These notes are colorful, contain watermarks, have national seals imbedded in them, and most importantly have photos of esteemed African leaders emblazoned upon them. The backs of some of the notes have pictures of the actual reserve banks of the respective nation that are architecturally unique mega-structures with landscaping and statues in front of them. Others have panoramic views of an African University complete with casually dressed African students and University regents/professors dressed in University regalia. Contrary to what the force has taught you, Africa is not a huge jungle of cannibalistic savages. Think about it, in terms of natural resources Africa is one of the richest continents on Earth, if not the richest, so the fact that they print their own money should not come as a surprise to you. Africa is a highly developed continent with rural, suburban, and urban areas just like America. There are forests, plains, mountains and wild animals just like America. There are also ATMs, the internet, DVDs, office buildings, factories, industrial parks, cell phones, cars, trucks, airports, planes, trains and automobiles just like America. Do not be fooled by the television which would have you believe that Africa is a continent full of HIV positive, undernourished people in continuous civil war with each other, because that simply is not true. Now does Africa have an AIDS issue? Yes, just like North America, South America, Europe and every other continent in the world. In fact, in recent years Russia and Eastern Europe have had the fastest rising rate of new HIV infections, but this fact is rarely publicized. If you do not believe it, go do your research on the internet and feel free to email me the results of your research at nqc@knowledgeofselfpublishing.com. Now, are certain places in Africa currently experiencing civil war? Yes, just like Ireland, Ukraine, Kyrgyzstan, and other places all over the world. Remember, America had a pretty nasty civil war after winning its independence as well. If you are African or African American and depend solely on the force and the media to teach you about yourself, you would be forced to believe you are the descendant of ignorant savages, but as you have read that is the exact opposite of the truth.

What You Were Not Taught (The Truth)

All of these FACTS represent 'What You Were Not Taught' about the positive side of African history. Now, armed with another small piece of 'What You Were Not Taught', let's take a minute to revisit Figure 21, What You Were Taught during your formal education.

	European History	African History
Positive	EP EP EP EP EP EP EP EP EP EP EP EP EP EP EP EP EP EP	AP
Negative	EN EN EN	AN AN AN AN AN AN AN AN AN

Figure 51 Categorization of what we were taught.

During your formal education you were taught:

- ➤ Much about the positive attributes of European history (EP).
- ➤ Much about the negative attributes of African history (AN).
- ➤ Little about the negative attributes of European history (EN).
- ➤ Almost nothing about the positive attributes of African history (AP).

After reading the section of this text covering the negative attributes of European history (EN), your history education became a little more balanced as represented in the below figure:

123

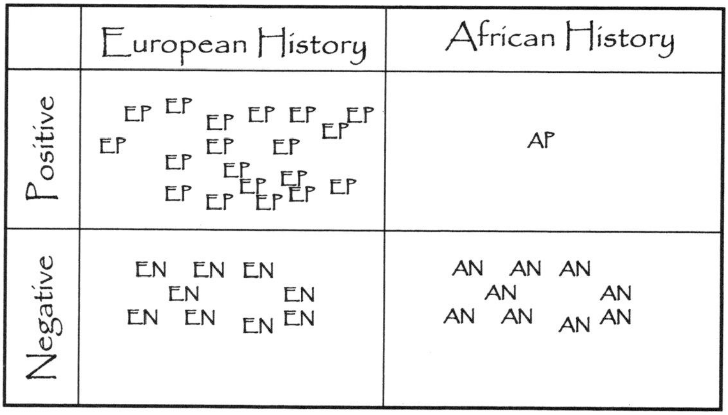

What You Were Not Taught (The Truth)

	European History	African History
Positive	EP EP EP EP EP EP EP EP EP EP EP EP EP EP EP EP EP EP	AP
Negative	EN EN EN EN EN EN EN EN EN	AN AN AN AN AN AN AN AN AN

Figure 52 Partial balancing of our education with the previously mentioned EN's added.

Learning of the negative attributes of European history added more ENs to your knowledge base, therefore beginning the process of balancing. Now that you have learned a piece of the countless positive facts of African history (AP), even more balance is created.

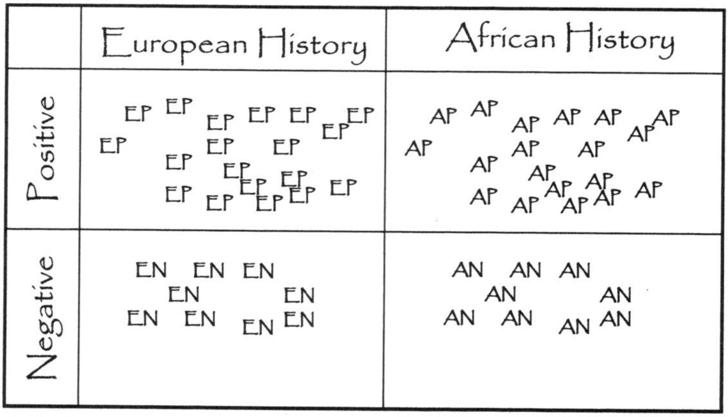

	European History	African History
Positive	EP EP EP EP EP EP EP EP EP EP EP EP EP EP EP EP EP EP	AP AP AP AP AP AP AP AP AP AP AP AP AP AP AP AP AP AP
Negative	EN EN EN EN EN EN EN EN EN	AN AN AN AN AN AN AN AN AN

Figure 53 A balanced education. Note that the European and African positives and negatives are equal.

124

What You Were Not Taught (The Truth)

After mapping the documented majesty of African ancestors, balance is achieved. Learning the positive historical occurrences of the African neutralizes the undeserving aura of inferiority created by only learning the negative facets of black people. This neutralization is accomplished by balancing the amount of negative African historical facts (AN) that you learned in school with the positive covered in this text (AP).

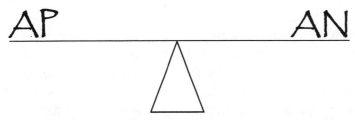

Figure 54 Notice the balance created by learning positive as well as negative aspects of African history.

You now realize that Africans and their descendants are not inferior to any other people of the world. You realize that they are humans who have done good and bad. You realize that people who share the African culture and their descendants are the same as people of many other cultures in the world, they have a negative side (AN) which the school system made sure you learned and they have a positive side which you have just read in the preceding pages. You know that like Europeans and European descendants, Africans have a very positive side of their history.

What You Were Not Taught (The Truth)

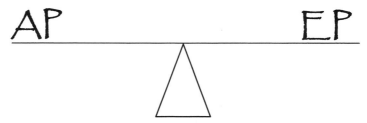

Figure 55 Notice the balance created by learning positive aspects of both African and European history.

The addition of some positive aspects of African history helps to complete the full matrix of truth. Each letter of each word counts as a weight in helping to balance your education. But why wasn't your education balanced to begin with? Why is American education so skewed towards European descendants? A proposed answer to that question is presented in the next chapter.

8. Why?

Our history curriculum focuses on history after European civilization. As proven, it also places unjustified attention on positive aspects of European history and negative aspects of African history. But why? Why was it decided you would not be taught all the facts covered in What You Were Not Taught and the thousands others not able to be addressed in this text? WHY? The full answer to this question is extremely complex but here are some contributing factors.

One contributing factor behind history's focus on post-European civilization is history as taught in this country was written by Europeans and people of European descent. Quite naturally, while writing the history books for everyone, the European American magnified his own accomplishments, therefore projecting the image of his culture above all others. Human nature forced Europeans to document and display their history in a positive light. Why would European historians focus on the time in history when they were barbarians, molesting young boys and eating their dead? Why would European historians highlight the incest, cannibalism and rampant

Why?

homicide practiced regularly by their ancestors?[1] What benefit would that present? Why would the man writing the history book focus on a period in time when his forefathers were savages and the forefathers of Africans were constructing majestic pyramids up to the heavens? What good is it for European historians to call attention to the archaeological evidence that points to the fact that their people were taught how to act in a civilized manner by ancient Africans whose descendants are not widely respected and routinely refer to themselves as niggers? On the surface, there is none. On the surface, there is no psychological or cultural benefit to this approach. The fact that Europeans wrote the history books helps explain why you were shown a prestigious marble statue of some Greek or Roman in a dignified pose and only told of his positive achievements; not that he ate his dying father, killed his mother, murdered a pregnant wife, killed his fellow man and made a coat from their skin, drank blood from his brother's skull, molested little boys, married his sister, murdered his brother, fed another man's son to him and claimed Egyptian knowledge as his own.

For Europeans to know and openly recognize that Africans created civilization and graciously passed it on to Europeans carries the psychological threat of influencing European descents to feel inferior to Africans and people of African descent. It seems some learned Europeans back in the annals of history came to the realization that presenting negative aspects of their history may cause their people to look negatively upon themselves and decided to do something about it. See, it is important to the ego of the white historian that the initial origins of man be white, black to be black, blue to be blue, orange to be orange, etc, Therefore, in order to protect the psyche of himself, his children and the whole of his people, these then learned Europeans rewrote history from their own perspective. They made it a point to steer the discipline of history to the point in time when Europeans controlled the civilized world and

128

Why?

effectively created an aura of mystery and uncertainty surrounding the period when Africans were the civilized world. This intellectual strategy for mental domination has allowed Europeans to maintain control of the civilized world to this day. Europeans continue to control the civilized world and thus they still control the perspective of history which has resulted in the gradual erasure or deliberate ignoring of history during the time when Africans had a firm control of the world and Europeans had yet to figure out how to protect themselves from the cold. But no matter how much a non-black person may will it false, eventually they have to come to terms with the fact that the remains of the first man was found in Africa, which makes the first man African.

It also seems that somewhere along the line another pioneering group of Europeans had yet another revelation. They observed the immense psychologically empowering benefits of the positive historical portrayal of their people and how it contributed to the Europeans ability to continue to dominate the world. They noticed how teaching Europeans that history started with Europeans seems to instill esteem in their collective selves. They also began to recognize that as more and more archaeologist performed more and more excavations in Africa, evidence of African glory documenting the African origin of civilization and the thousands of years when Africans dominated the civilized world became more prominent. They noticed that these archaeological finds would fuel the Africans' fire to finally step up and take the credit for establishing humanity on Earth. Therefore to douse that potential fire, the conclusion was had that the positive portrayal of European history coupled with the negative historical portrayal of Africans would have crippling psychological effects on African people that would allow the European to continue his political and financial dominance virtually uncontested and create a permanent aura of uncertainty about the African evidence founded. Also here is where the wide spread erasure and defacing of artifacts that documented African

129

Why?

domination began. Distinct African facial features of colossal African statues i.e. the wide noses and full lips, were blown off to hide the fact that Africans lived so comfortably, were so powerful and enjoyed the material resources, physical resources, technical knowledge, time and civilization to build colossal monuments in honor of their kings. The hardcore evidence documenting the advanced status of African culture was intentionally defiled to mentally dominate the black mind for generations! Also, this strategy of mental domination permanently created an aura of uncertainty around African greatness. In the end, the period in history often referred to the lost civilization would be more accurately described as the erased civilization. The truth was erased and replaced with wild delusions of white Africans or Europeans temporarily moving to Africa, establishing civilization and then disappearing into thin air. White Africans, aliens building the pyramids, lost civilizations, etc. were all manufactured products of this strategy to mask the truth. As wild as these claims were, unfortunately they were successful. There seems to be a permanent aura of mystery that surrounds ancient African history created by these men. Despite remaining artifacts and hieroglyphics etched in stone on temple and pyramid walls, this aura of mystery still thrives. It is simply amazing how documentaries, books and movies about billion year old dinosaurs can be made without the slightest hint of doubt about their billon year old existence. It is exponentially amazing how the existence of civilized humans who lived only thousands of years ago and wrote their history down is mysterious or lost. Dinosaurs' species, life span, migrations, social patterns, diet, height, weight, etc. can be told with absolute certainty, but the period when Africans ruled only a few thousand years ago is a big mystery! It is certain that a T-Rex ate 50 little dinosaurs a week, took 3 dumps a day, and migrated south for the winter, but mystical and mysterious that King Tut pictured on the front of this book was black! Utterly ridiculous!

Why?

The history of Egypt is a major piece of the glorious past of Africans. It is not the only piece as Western Kingdoms had significant accomplishments as well, but it is a major piece. Over time, there has been a general attempted separation of Egypt from Africa. The 'white Africans' message has spread far and wide as the train of thought that there were whites who moved to Africa and developed civilization in the Nile Valley still lingers today as proved in movies and television programs about ancient Egypt. The actors cast in the African roles are mostly white, some mixed, or in some cases very light skinned African Americans. You never see velvety, deep dark-skinned African Americans or Africans in these roles. Even the History Channel presents these ancient Africans as a light skinned, kind of in between mixed race instead of pure African blooded people of the past. Why? Is it because this mysterious race of white blacks actually existed and lived in Africa during that period and has since disappeared? Is it because no dark skinned actors were available to play these roles? Or is it because the writers and directors of these programs and movies who are of European descent, fell victim to their human need of self-pride, self-esteem and self-worth and also victimized by the force, naturally wrote, directed and cast their films from the dominant European perspective? In fact, the only dark skinned ancient Egyptian role portrayal I can recall is the Michael Jackson *Remember the Time* music video. In this video, many Egypt, Africa characters were cast as powerful, very dark-skinned, full lipped, broad nosed people of African descent, starring Eddie Murphy as the pharaoh and Imani as his royal wife. The reasoning behind the casting of dark-skinned as Egyptians is someone involved with the production of the video had the consciousness and knowledge of themself to portray the African American perspective. The powerful African American entertainers involved with this video (Eddie Murphy, Earvin "Magic" Johnson, Imani, or Jackson himself), and/or some producer, writer, etc. assisted in

131

Why?

presenting the video from the African American perspective. And while *Remember The Time* was just a music video, it is extremely important in what it represents. It represents the other perspective that must be represented to begin the balancing.

Understand, this bias and false train of thought portrayed in many forms of media and academics that suggest Egyptians were white or otherwise separate from the rest of Africa represents the separation of Egypt from the rest of Africa. It represents the separation of African descendents from their heritage and the separation of people of African descent from themselves. People of African descent, African Americans in particular, need to openly recognize that Egyptian history is African history and make other people accept the fact that Egypt is Africa and Africa is Egypt. Why? The eternal connection of Africa to Egypt and Egypt to Africa is necessary to counter any ploys to deprive people of African descent of a significant piece of their glorious past. The same way you cannot separate the history of Washington, D.C. from the history of the United States, you cannot separate the history of Egypt from the history of Africa. Egyptians are Africans. Many authors, historians and professors speak of Egypt as if a separate entity from Africa. In actuality Egypt is part of Africa's whole and therefore Egyptians represent the African people and the African continent. As some historians discovered the developments Egypt passed on to the rest of the world, they then attempted to interpret and explain the history of Egypt as separate from Africa with the intent to disconnect Egypt's greatness from the rest of the so-called "dark continent". Do not be fooled. Egypt is Africa and Africa is Egypt.

It would not be logical for the European who has rousted control of the civilized world from Africans, beginning with Cambyses II, to turn around and teach the conquered Africans about the period in time when they dominated Europeans. In fact, it would be completely logical for the previously conquered European to teach the African and his descendents that he never

Why?

has been and never will be, while simultaneously brainwashing the general population with the opinion Europeans and his descendents are, were and always will be. These teachings represent the basic ingredients to the formula of modern day education that generates the best niggas money can buy. The curriculum (via the teachers) subliminally whispers to the African American child, 'your people are underachievers, with the exception of a few, so it is quite alright for you to underachieve as well. As a matter-of-fact, the world expects you to underachieve'. The strategy of mental domination and ploy of African American inferiority seems to have been a calculated and obviously extremely effective strategy since Europeans continue to dominate the civilized world. But any logical and sane person must accept the evidence that proves civilization began in Africa. After that acceptance, their perspective as determined by their experience, education and environment impacts the interpretation and explanation of that fact.

The focus of this text is to expose the deceit in your education and provide instruction on how to correct it, not to develop some big conspiracy theory of who inserted deception in your education. From this author's perspective, the majority of the African American population on a whole has been suckered, swindled, got, bent over, scammed, punked, hoodwinked and bamboozled as most have fell victim to the myth that they came from nothing, are nothing and will never be anything. Visit any major city in the country, go to the most rundown neighborhood in the city and tell me the skin color of its inhabitants. The arrest of the African American mind is the ultimate hustle, the greatest scam in the history of the world! The almighty force effortlessly holds people of African descent down while simultaneously teaching them to hold each other down. Identifying a conspirator of today's biased education is not important. Spending hours out of your life expending energy and wasting precious time attempting to identify a perpetrator of this

133

Why?

crime of humanity is a complete waste. Yesterday was yesterday and today is today, but tomorrow is a new day waiting to be influenced by your actions. See, it does not really matter if the chicken came before the egg or vice versa. What matters is all of our brains are scrambled. Our education is flipped and presented white sunny side up which aides European Americans in getting over easy and African Americans hard-boiled. But read on, for instruction on how to acquire a nutritious, balanced education, true and full history that is absolutely necessary for a positive adjustment of your mentality.

Part D: *The Whole Truth…*
The Solution

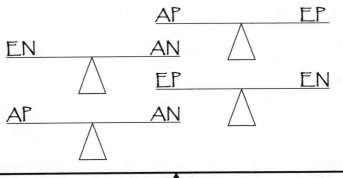

9. *True & Full History*

How infuriating it is to discover that historians, archaeologists, professors and so-called experts have either accidentally or intentionally filtered the story of mankind to develop inferiority and superiority complexes in their fellow human brothers and sisters. Please be aware that an unfiltered, true and full history of the world and its people does exist! It is now your task to transform your new found furor into fuel and use this fuel to power your mental vehicle towards a true and full history. This true and full history provides both the graceful and disgraceful history of all people. It is not biased, is not filtered and most importantly it reveals the magnificent accomplishments of Africans and people of African descent as well as the low points in the history of Europeans and people of European descent to create balance in what you were taught about the history of white and black people.

Due to the brainwashing nature of today's curriculum, many Americans will flat out refuse to believe that a magnificent history of Africans and a shameful history of Europeans even exist. Typically, a person's level of formal education will be the deciding factor in determining their ultimate receptiveness to true history. Whether through coincidence or by design, those who are most receptive to true and full history have the least resources to attain and promote it. Conversely, those who are the least receptive to the full history of man have the full resources to attain and promote it. The attainment, admission and promotion of the full history of all people will balance the scale of each cultures' past accomplishments and embarrassments, thus creating a balance among the cultures. The attainment and promotion of true and full history of the world must begin with you. Course-by-course, teacher-by-teacher, historian-by-historian, author-by-author, book-by-book, word-by-word, letter-by-letter you must strive to gain a full history of the world. You already have the European and European American perspective down, it is what you learned your entire life. The perspective that is missing is the African and African American perspective. You must take courses and read books taught and written from the African and African American perspective (a list of these authors will be provided later in this text).

The attainment of true and full history will lead you directly towards Knowledge of Self. Both European Americans and African Americans need a solid knowledge of themselves and knowledge of each other to promote true equality. Teaching that blacks and whites are historical equals will perpetuate society toward the realization that we are presently equal. Currently, we are taught whites are historically superior to blacks but were eventually convinced to treat blacks as equals by Abraham Lincoln, the Emancipation Proclamation, the 13th, 14th 15th amendments, Martin Luther King Jr., etc. We were taught the natural order of man is white over black and then whites were coerced or convinced to recognize blacks as equals via men's laws. The inherent error of using this method is that it gives whites as individuals the choice of treating blacks equally or not. It gives them the choice of following their misperceived

138

natural law (white over black) or man's law (should treat equally anyway). As we all very well know, some whites choose to follow their misperceived natural law while others happily follow man's law. This creates confusion because in today's politically conscious environment it is difficult for blacks to tell which whites follow the misperceived natural law and which follow man's law. It was not that difficult in the 30's, 40's, 50's and 60's because social behavior allowed Americans to voice their true beliefs without consequence, but that is not the case today. White's option to choose as created by biased history education subsequently pressures some blacks to constantly lobby white Americans to follow man's law and treat them equally. This lobbying manifests itself in the form of civil rights actions, marches, court cases, etc. It makes other blacks want to leave this country (back to Africa movements) despite all they have invested and leaves others with a crippling feeling of incompleteness.

History as taught in our country creates the whites' option to choose and judge blacks. If we teach true and full history that honestly depicts blacks and whites as natural equals, the necessity for whites to choose is eliminated. Natural law as defined in history class would say whites and blacks are equals which coincides with man's law. A true and full history puts everyone on notice that blacks and whites were natural equals from the very beginning which eliminates anyone from having any choice in the matter. Everyone would be taught that blacks and whites WERE and ARE EQUALS, all members of the human race. By all people learning a true, full and balanced history and therefore attaining knowledge of themselves and knowledge of each other, all people learn that blacks dominated whites, whites dominated blacks, whites had black slaves, blacks had white slaves, some blacks were savages, some whites were savages and most importantly the equality of all men and women is justified by natural law. All people would learn that we all come from the same parents in Africa. The perception of natural law would coincide with man's law and with the passing of a few generations the 'race problem' in America could be greatly reduced.

It is easy to recognize the benefit of African Americans attainment of true and full history, but what benefit would it be for Europeans to now go back and introduce those negative aspects into their history which is currently portrayed in such a positive manner? You read earlier that <u>on the surface</u> those Europeans who wrote history had no motivation to focus on the negative side of their history as it brought no psychological or cultural benefit to their people. <u>On the surface</u>, the same applies for today's Europeans. Why insert the negative, especially since history makes them out to be the heroes of the world? If it ain't broke, don't fix it right? Wrong. It is broke. It creates the psychological threat of making blacks feel inferior and also condemns whites to repeating mistakes made by their forefathers. Beneath the surface, there is a massive benefit, a full knowledge of themselves! KNOWLEDGE OF SELF is the one overwhelming benefit to identify the negative as well as the positive. The Europeans full knowledge of themselves will allow them to better understand some instances of their bizarre behavior today and gives them the ability to avoid making the same mistakes their ancestors made. Promoting these negative aspects will let Europeans know what is in the other half of their blood, because a person, white, black, green or purple cannot hide what is in their blood. Learning of the Romans assassinations of their leaders will give you a better understanding of why our American leaders were assassinated or suffered attempted assassinations. Learning that Europeans stole African knowledge in 325 B.C. allows you to better understand why Europeans stole Africans in 1400 A.D. It was in their blood. Learning that Europeans were cannibals who thought it more honorable to eat their dying instead of burying them allows you to better understand the actions of Jeffrey Dahmer who ate humans. Once you learned that cannibalism was a common European practice, you then can understand the actions of Jeffrey a little better. If you knew that eating the dying is an old European tradition, then you would understand that Jeffrey is simply carrying on tradition. He was just doing what was in his genetic make-up to do. The same goes for Ed Gein who Hollywood modeled *The Silence of the Lamb*'s Buffalo Bill after. Once you learn that Scynthians used to make human skin coats from their victims' skin, you better understand that the genes in Ed Gein's blood told him to make human skin clothes from his victims' skin. John Haigh, who is known as the acid bath murderer, would kill his victims, drink their blood then disintegrate their bodies in acid. Once you learn of the Europeans genocide and drinking of each others blood, you understand John Haigh was simply carrying on European tradition. You better understand the European tradition of swinging couples once you learn that the Massagetae men made their wives available to one another. After you learn Constantine murdered much of his family, you better understand why so many European and European American men kill their families. The genocide trait or cultural characteristic was simply passed down through their blood. Being formally introduced to the negative side of their history allows European Americans to have a better understanding of these actions, but more importantly having the better understanding affords them the opportunity to formally address the issues. Through true and full history and a complete knowledge of themselves, they get the opportunity to avoid their forefathers' mistakes. It is no different than the son of an alcoholic learning what's in his blood (alcoholism) and gaining the opportunity to formally address his unbelievable urge to drink. By knowing that his father was an alcoholic, he gains the opportunity to learn from his father's mistakes and advance his family up the evolutional ladder.

True & Full History

African Americans also stand to benefit immensely from a true and full history which will give them knowledge of themselves. Their number one benefit will be Mr. Booker T. Washington's proclamation of being able to advance their African American culture through the power of their ancestry, which has been addressed numerous times throughout this text. They can learn from the actions of the pharaohs, kings and queens; that they belong in elevated financial, political and social positions in the world as they once were and not just as niggers in American culture. But during that voyage towards the universal advancement of their culture, there will be other incidental benefits of true and full history for the African American, one being a better understanding of their general materialism and attraction to flashiness, gaudiness a.k.a. bling. Through true and full history, African Americans will learn that they come from the richest of all continents, Africa, and that their ancestors thrived off the continent's natural resources such as gold, diamonds, etc. This information will give them the opportunity to recognize that in Africa the land provided the bling while in America the bling is provided by European, Chinese and Jewish-American retailers, wholesalers and distributors. Their inherent want for these material items was passed from their ancestors through the blood. By being conscious of their history they gain the opportunity to realize their inherent nature and address the exploitation of their want by American capitalists. They can learn how the institution of religion, lagging technological advancements, too much trust and too little skepticism destroyed ancient African cultures and they can gain the opportunity to learn from their ancestors' mistakes. Most importantly African Americans must gain knowledge of themselves to close the wide gaps in education, economics, poverty and health. True and full history must be utilized by the African American to reverse the expectation of their youth from low expectation of success-high expectation of failure to high expectation of success-no expectation of failure.

Overall, all people must use true and full history to create equality among all and avoid making the same mistakes of the past. True and full history will move us away from superior-inferior, majority-minority, we-them concept and toward the truth – we are all members of the human race who practice different cultures. The saying goes, it is insanity to take the same path twice and expect a different result. Well without true and full history and a complete knowledge of oneself, you are destined to take the same path twice, thusly falling into a generational looping pattern of skewed perception and causing the past to repeat itself just as the world spins on its axis. You will find that it will be easier for some to acquire knowledge of themselves and forward their culture than others. Depending upon a person's background, they will be more or less receptive to the concept of true and full history. Read on to see where you stand.

10. *Receptiveness to True & Full History*

Different categories of Americans see the concept of true and full history through different eyes and from totally different perspectives. Americans in certain categories will be more receptive to the idea of full history than Americans in other categories. The determining factor in the degree of receptiveness to the full history concept is an individual's level of formal education. In this country there exist three levels of formal education: an individual with an above average education; an individual with an average education; and an individual with a below average education. The three levels of formal education are defined as follows:

1. Above Average Education - An individual with an above average education (abbreviated A.A.E.) has a high school diploma and a Bachelor's, Master's or Doctorate degree.

2. Average Education - An individual with an average education (abbreviated A.E.) has a high school diploma

and/or an Associate's Degree or a trade school professional certificate.

3. Below Average Education - An individual with a below average education (abbreviated B.A.E.) attended high school but does not have a high school diploma. Those individuals with a general education diploma (G.E.D.) also fall in the B.A.E. category.[1]

Please note these descriptors refer to the level of formal education an individual has attained. The descriptors (Above, Average and Below) is not representative of how smart a person is nor of their level of intelligence. A person's intelligence is not directly correlated or directly linked to their level of formal education. For example, a person with a Below Average Education (B.A.E.) can very well have a high level of intelligence and a person with an Above Average Education (A.A.E.) can be of very low intelligence. These descriptors are used to demonstrate that the longer an individual attended school, the longer they have been subjected to the force. The longer an individual's subjection to the force, the longer they have been brainwashed to believe whites are everything and blacks are nothing. The longer an individual has been brainwashed, the less receptive they will be to the idea of a full history and the thought that blacks are everything as well.

Knowledge is received to the brain via an individual's mind's eye a.k.a. the third eye. The concept of the brain and the third eye is no different than the concept of a computer (mind) and a scanner (third eye). The same way the computer is filled with data via images read by the scanner, the mind is filled with knowledge through formal education and conscious living through its third eye. The skewed and biased history of man as taught today is garbage, clutter, fodder that manipulates perception using biased information.

Receptiveness to True & Full History

Figure 56 Your third eye or your mind's eye.

These distorted teachings clog the vision of the mind's eye the same way dust, lint and filth would cloud any images read by the scanner. The greater amount of biased formal education an individual receives equals an increased amount of garbage in their brain that impairs the vision of their mind's eye, ultimately making them less receptive to a full history, the truth. The less biased formal education an individual receives equals less garbage in their brain which allows a clearer mind's eye, ultimately increasing their reception to a full and true history of themselves. See pictorial view below for further explanation:

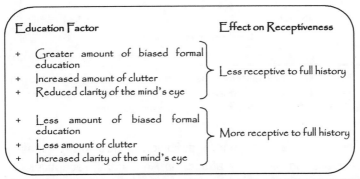

Figure 57 Effect of biased formal education on reception to full unbiased history.

Receptiveness to True & Full History

Additionally, the older an individual is the more set in their beliefs and ways they are. If a person learned and witnessed manifestations of black inferiority and white superiority their whole lives, they will be less receptive to a true and full history. The opposite will be true for those older persons who witnessed true equality among all people their whole life.

Ultimately, the clarity of the mind's eye or third eye is directly related to the level of biased formal education an individual has received. So an individual with an A.A.E. has received the greatest level of biased education; has little to no clarity of the third eye; and is the least receptive to true and full history. On the other hand, an individual with a B.A.E. has received the least amount of biased education; has a clear third eye; and consequently is the most receptive to true and full history.

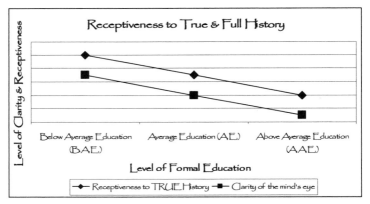

Figure 58 In most cases receptiveness to true and full history will be directly related to the clarity of the third eye. There will always be anomalies (ex: an individual with an A.A.E. in African Studies) but most will fit the bill.

The above serves as a general definition of how today's biased formal education generally affects all Americans' receptiveness to full history. Once individual and group perspectives are taken into consideration, there are variations of European American and African American cultures receptiveness to full history.

European Americans and Receptiveness of FULL History

European Americans with an above average (A.A.E) and average (A.E) formal education really have heard all they need to hear in the classroom to walk around with their collective chins up and chests out. The biased curriculum has convinced them that they have created it all, ran it all and done it all. Today's formal education screams to European Americans that they are it (period). They learn of the "World's First Awards" and everything else from the dominant European perspective. Eventually, 18-26 years of proactively studying the subliminal message of white superiority that is mixed in with today's education permanently blurs the vision of their third eye. The European American with A.A.E. and A.E. can no longer envision any significant accomplishments of any other people. Their third eye can only accept the significant accomplishments of white people.[2]

While B.A.E. European Americans are not subject to the filth of today's education that clogs the mind's eye for as long as A.A.E. and A.E. European Americans are, their mind's eye still becomes clouded through other avenues controlled by European Americans. The concept of white superiority portrayed on television, printed on paper, verbally passed through word-of-mouth and talk radio combined with a natural feeling of self-worth are enough to persuade the B.A.E. European American to close their mind's eye to any forms of non-European American greatness. Ultimately, the majority of European Americans are floating around noses high, shoulders back, reeling with confidence as they have been convinced they are the creators of everything and rulers of the earth. The superiority complex is expressed more intensely by older European Americans with

Receptiveness to True & Full History

A.A.E. and A.E. (remember the age affect), but still expressed to some degree by the vast majority of European Americans nonetheless. They have no interest whatsoever in the rest of history, his-story, her-story, their-story nor our-story. Their mind's eye is totally clogged with garbage and the lid of the mind's eye is voluntarily closed. There is no light for A.A.E. and A.E. European Americans to seek out as they have already been taught the light in the form of white-washed history of the world as presented in any typical classroom and the B.A.E. European Americans have absorbed it through other means. They have no reason to ponder the TRUE HISTORY of the African American or themselves as the current version they learned places their people in the grandest of positions. Mention the concept of the African Origin of Civilization to 100 European Americans and see what response you get. In fact, feel free to send me your findings at nqc@knowledgeofselfpublishing.com. What you will find is on the whole European Americans are the least receptive to true and full history.

African Americans and Receptiveness of FULL History

The African American with an A.A.E. typically does not have the slightest idea of his/her FULL HISTORY. His extended formal education and consequent subjection to years of psychological conditioning that he is the descendant of jungle bunnies and slaves clogs the vision of his mind's eye and prevents it from seeing the truth. The third eye of an African American with just an A.E. is a little less clogged with the poison of a formal education, but he is too busy either swimming in contentment with his position or just trying to get by that the opportunity to delve into the truth rarely arises. Now, the African American with a B.A.E. has the clearest mind's eye (third eye) of all the above as he has taken in the least of the poisonous formal education. While somewhat clogged with visions of European American domination via other avenues (media, etc.), he has not been subjected to the years of out-right repetitive psychological conditioning and brainwashing as other African and European Americans with a higher level of formal education have. Since he has not been subjected to years of psychological conditioning, he is able to dismiss, to a certain extent, the negative portrayal of himself and his people received through those other avenues. Unlike the B.A.E. European American, the other avenues of learning that portray the African American in a negative light goes against their basic feeling of self-worth. Since these other mediums do not have the authority of formal titles (professor, doctor) and are portraying the B.A.E. African American against what nature has instilled in him, he is somewhat able to shake that clutter from his mind's eye. As a result, his mind would be the most receptive to the idea of the African Pharaoh Narmer smiting blue-eyed, blond-haired barbarians from north of Africa. Unfortunately, the majority of African Americans in this category have little power as they are trapped in the gutters of American ghettos and prisons and have neither the leisure nor resources of attaining such 'controversial' knowledge.

Maybe through some God-instilled mechanism of self-preservation, African Americans with B.A.E. realized the poison they were receiving through their formal education, recognized the gradual clogging of their mind's eye and made a conscious decision to stop going to school to protect their third eye? Maybe, just maybe this is the exact reason why so many blacks chose to quit school. Maybe there is a link between the low academic achievement scores of African Americans and the negative portrayal of their people in history books? Maybe some of these young brothers and sisters value the health of their third eye above their formal education. Unfortunately, this theoretical value structure causes financial stagnation and they become stuck in the ghettoes and prisons of America. They successfully protect their third eye but consequently expose their uneducated behinds to a society that is taught to fear them. It is this vast majority of B.A.E. African Americans who are the most receptive to the concept of full history as they have succeeded in protecting their third eye, but without an education or a means to prosper, they have the least resources to attain true history.

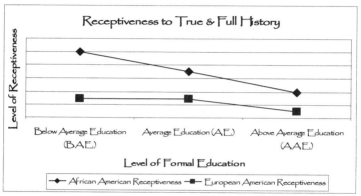

Figure 59 In general African Americans will be more receptive to true and full history since it appeals to their natural feeling of self-worth. The B.A.E. African American will be the most receptive to true and full history.

The Irony

Ironically, but not coincidentally, A.A.E. and A.E. Americans who are the least receptive to the full truth have both the leisure and resources necessary to dedicate towards learning the full truth. Unfortunately, the clogging or closing of their mind's eye with the poison of today's education prevents the thought. Even more ironic, highly educated African Americans who operate in the European American dominated corporate world have the greatest need to know their full history but are least receptive of all African Americans to its existence. Everyday, they are competing with a sea of European Americans fully charged with the biased knowledge of themselves. The confidence of believing that Europeans developed the world is all they need to act as though the world owes them a favor. On the other hand, African Americans with no knowledge of themselves are stuck forcing themselves oft-times to work twice as hard for the same pay and playing the overall slave role, since that is the role they leaned from every social studies book read from 1st grade to 12th grade. A.A.E. African Americans who operate in the European American dominated corporate world absolutely require the knowledge of full history in order to defend themselves and their people while in general conversations with European Americans. Current education has taught African Americans and European Americans alike that the history of the African American is savage and sorry. So when an example of African American inferiority is pointed out in the form of some historical piece of information portrayed from a European perspective or some movie scene portrayed from a European perspective, the A.A.E. African American is left defenseless. He is unable to oppose the portrayal of his people's inferiority because neither he nor his European counterpart is familiar with true & full history. It is at this critical point where A.A.E. African Americans need knowledge of self to defend themselves and their people by countering the negative skewed thought with true and full history. Unfortunately, more times than not, the A.A.E. African American will not be able to intelligently retaliate as his low reception to the idea of full history prevented him from considering it. The same is true when some historical fact presented from the European American perspective that supports the belief of white superiority is pointed out. Again, both have been taught that blacks are nothing and whites are everything, so neither party is able to negate the point which simply serves to reinforce the false conception. In fact, it is more likely that the A.A.E. African American will agree with the skewed perspective as it was drilled in their head during the 16-20 years of their formal education.

153

Receptiveness to True & Full History

At the end of the day, what you have is those who have been conditioned by the force not to seek the truth has the means to attain it and those who would be most receptive to the truth do not have the means to attain it. It is a very vicious cycle of inferiority that must be broken starting with you. The fact that you are almost finished reading this text is proof positive that you are on your way. Now comes the solution, specific instructions on what you must do to get there!

11. *The Solution*

Here is your task. You, be you black, white, blue or green, must balance your education.

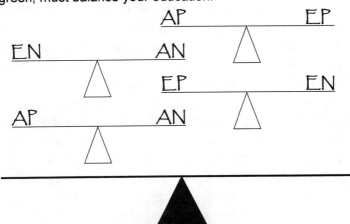

Figure 60 Your goal is a fully balanced education!

In order to erase the perception that whites are super-human you must balance the overwhelming positivity surrounding their history (EP) via the addition of negativity (EN), as difficult and uncomfortable as that may be. To erase the perception that blacks are sub-human, you must balance the overwhelming negativity surrounding blacks' history (AN) via the addition of positivity (AP). You must balance the historical facts that portray whites as superior with some historical facts that portray whites as inferior. You must balance the historical facts that portray blacks as inferior with some historical facts that portray blacks as superior. To create equality in society, you must create equality in history. You have to balance the historical fact that Africans were dominated by others with historical facts about when Africans dominated others. You have to balance the historical fact Europeans dominated others with historical facts about when Europeans were dominated.

A true, full and balanced history is your goal. There are two paths that lead to the goal, a long term path and a short term path, and both are paved with books. You must learn the African and African American perspective of history as written by any historian, but particularly written by African and African American historians! GET STARTED TODAY! DON'T PUT OFF, PROCRASTINATE, POSTPONE OR HESITATE!

In the long run, one would hope that the Department of Education and school systems throughout America will one day equally implement the African and African American perspective into the standard curriculum, therefore creating balance in the force. African Americans are essential Americans and deserve to be taught the positive aspects of their history in their country; their country that was built with their blood, sweat and tears. Understand, the source of America's worldly power is its phenomenal economic muscle; and that economic muscle was developed with slave money. Billions of African and African American man-hours spent performing hard labor without compensation is the financial foundation that America stands on today. Those hours spent are what allow America to dominate

The Solution

the world today. Imagine being the owner of a business and all of your employees work for free; you don't pay them any salary, you don't provide any benefits, they don't get lunch breaks, and work 14 hours a day, every day. Why, in no time you would be filthy rich. Well, imagine reaping the financial profits of this business for 300 years. That is the African American sacrifice. They forcefully donated their salary and benefits for 300 years for the benefit of our nation. And for that reason alone the promotion of the positive side of their history in the school system is owed, just a small reimbursement for years of their forefathers' hard work. But in reality, one should not expect the school system to teach it. Hopefully it will happen, but do not hold your breath, and more importantly you absolutely cannot beg for it. Even if one day down the line the force is balanced, African Americans should not totally rely on the same entity that once created specific laws punishing your fathers if they tried to learn how to read and write with providing every aspect of your education. Unfortunately, not enough generations of humans have passed to purge the hatred of that era, and in this author's opinion it would take thousands of years for the purging to complete. Even though the administrators of the entity have changed and the times have changed dramatically, you still will be required to supplement your education. One would be a fool to receive 100% of their education from an entity that a little over a hundred years ago considered them 3/5ths human on paper and in practice did not consider them human at all. Simply not enough generations have passed.

In the short run, African Americans must take the self-initiative to learn for themselves. You must supplement your education and your children's education with the information necessary to create balance.[1] The first step of this supplemented education is READING!! Acquire any book written by any of the following historians to propel yourself towards knowledge of self:

The Solution

Dr. John Henrik Clarke, Dr. Yosef ben-Jochannan, Dr. Cheikh Anta Diop, Dr. George G. M. James, Dr. Chancellor Williams, Dr. Ivan Van Sertima, Joel A. Rogers, Dr. W. E. B. DuBois, Indus Khamit-Kush, J.C. Degraft-Johnson, Professor John G. Jackson, Dr. Na'iam Akbar, Dr. Molefi Kete Asante, John Hope Franklin, C.L.R. James, Basil Davidson, Dr. Frances Cress Welsing, Dr. Ishakamusa Barashango, Martin R. Delany, Dr. Carter G. Woodson, Marcus Garvey, Dr. Asa G. Hilliard, Dr. Jacob Carruthers, Lerone Bennett, Jr., A. Phillip Randolph, Dr. Leonard Jeffries, Dr. Maulana Karenga, Dr. Amos N. Wilson, William Leo Hansberry, Gerald Massey, Alain Locke, Runoko Rashidi, Dr. Columbus Salley, David Walker, Dr. Cornel West, Henry Highland Garnett, E. Franklin Frazier, William Monroe Trotter, Ida B. Wells-Barnett, Roy Wilkins, Dr. Kenneth B. Clark, Arthur Schomburg

These women and men have written hundreds of books, essays, and speeches necessary to balance your education. Their books are readily available and waiting to fill you with the truth. One book at a time, you must gain knowledge of yourself to provide you with the inspiration and expectation to excel. Additionally, the publisher of this text is dedicated towards the aggressive promotion of the African and African American perspective of history and life so please look out for future titles dedicated towards filling you with the truth. Aggressively learn the rest of 'What You Were Not Taught'. Just because you were not taught it, does not mean you cannot learn it. See, this is America, and we are Americans, free to learn whatever we want to learn. Granted this was not the case a few hundred years ago, but it certainly is the case now. The same way you are free to learn the latest line dance and exercise your newly developed skill in the club, you are free to learn true and full history, knowledge of self and exercise your knowledge in the world. The same way you are free to buy liquor, cigarettes, fast food, DVDs and CDs that can tear down your physical and mental states, you are also free to buy books that will increase the knowledge of yourself and give you the confidence to attain financial, political and social strength. You must develop your cognitive abilities, be able to think for yourself to avoid the blind acceptance of facts presented from one perspective as the whole truth. Learn and respect the African and African American perspective.

During your completion of the first step (Reading) you must take time to consciously analyze your receptiveness to true and full history. You must RECOGNIZE and be conscious of the influence your environment, education, experiences and state of your mind's eye may have on your receptiveness to the truth and make any adjustments necessary to fully embrace the truth. You have years of psychological conditioning to break, and it will be very difficult to do so. Just know, nothing worthwhile is easy and anything worthwhile takes pure, unadulterated WORK. To help your transition, you must network with others. Read the writings of the authors listed with friends or with study groups. Email me at nqc@knowledgeofselfpublishing.com for help or coordination with others in your area.

After you as an individual or group have read true and full history and are able to accept it, you must then RECIPROCATE 'What You Were Not Taught' along to your peers, friends, foes and family, especially your children. The earlier you insert the African American perspective into your childrens' lives (or into the lives of any children if you do not have any of your own), the easier it will be for them to accept the truth (remember the negative effects time and age has on receptiveness). By introducing 'What You Were Not Taught' early in their lives, you prevent the youth from ever inheriting the

The Solution

skewed perspective of the force effectively breaking the vicious cycle of attempted inferiority in people of color. You must reciprocate to the youth 'What You Were Not Taught' which is now what they are not being taught. If the youth in your life have already been negatively influenced by the force then raise their awareness with this text. Help them see the light in the same manner I hopefully have helped you. Since you are now aware, identify the fallacy in their lessons when you help them with homework and help to develop their perspective. You must reciprocate the knowledge, through not only your children, but your parents, siblings, nieces, nephews, grandparents, uncles, aunts, cousins, neighbors, friends, people in the city, people in the suburbs, people out in the country, people living above the poverty line, people living below the poverty line, cops, inmates, realtors, government employees, painters, plumbers, lawyers, doctors, Muslims, Christians, Jews, Buddhists, black, white, red and yellow humans all over the world. Think about the African American perspective, study it, talk about it and most importantly, be about it. Organize, hold and/or attend discussion groups in person and especially on the internet. Knowledge of self makes a very interesting topic of discussion at dinner parties, family reunions, the water cooler, at home and abroad.

The Solution

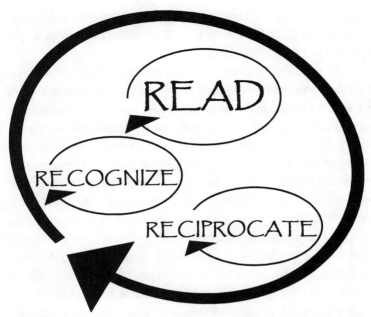

Figure 61 You must READ true and full history, RECOGNIZE your receptiveness
and aggressively RECIPROCATE it to the world, starting in your household!

You must learn:
What you were not taught and
Apply this knowledge to
Negate the
Negativity you were taught.

You must learn:
    We
    Ain't
    No
    Niggas!!

The Solution

While reading, you must recognize and continually reciprocate the fact that We Ain't No Niggas! with intense conviction to the rest of ourselves and the rest of the world.

After attaining knowledge of yourself, then what will you do? What is the point? Booker T. Washington revealed the point to us in 1900. African Americans must use the true and full history of our ancestry, the knowledge of ourselves to forward our race. That is the point. We must use the accomplishments of our forefathers as standards and the goal of each generation is to raise the standard or raise the proverbial bar for the next generation. We must raise our political, social and especially financial position in our country. You must use the positive accomplishments of your African family to boost your esteem to new heights, then utilize the positive energy radiating off your esteem to build and ultimately create equality and wealth. As an example, my people in the city, once you have knowledge of self, you will realize the inequitable relationship between yourself and the Chinese-Americans who have set up stores in your neighborhood. You will realize the total disrespect they show for our people when they set up a store, automatically place a three inch glass between themselves and you but leave a slot just big enough for you to slide your money underneath. Blatant disrespect. They do not employ any people in the community, do not send their kids to the neighborhood schools, do not heat the part of the store on the other side of the glass, and do not buy anything from African Americans. When you have knowledge of yourself, you realize that the Chinese culture is not better than the African culture and that Chinese man has no right to treat you in such a disrespectful manner. Use the knowledge of yourself to make that Chinese man treat you with respect, to create equality. Tell him, the first man was born in Africa, therefore the first Chinese man was a variant of the African, then tell him that because of this fact, he must show you respect. Then use your new found esteem and confidence to make others

The Solution

in your community aware of this unbalanced situation and then develop a strategy to open your own store where you will respect your customers (your people) and create wealth. Young professional - use the knowledge of yourself to make your middle-class European American co-workers respect your culture. Whenever some historical fact, scene from a movie or story reported on the news from the dominant European perspective highlight some negative piece of African American culture, drop some gems from 'What You Were Not Taught' on them. Refer them to *We Ain't No Niggas!* and www.knowledgeofselfpublishing.com so they can read the truth for themselves. Identifying these historical facts that call out the positive and negative sides of both blacks and whites almost forces them to see the equality among different cultures of the human race. Identify the EN and AP to create balance in their brains or at least get them to think about it. Being deceived into believing you are nothing but a nigga pushes you to act niggerish (feel sorry for yourself, pessimistic attitude, feel like you belong on the bottom in a struggle), but knowing that greatness is in your blood allows you to do great things. Learning that you came from greatness motivates you to become great, and it all starts with reading. Here is what I want you to do; hold this book in your left hand; raise your right hand and read aloud 'I pledge to dedicate at least 4 hours every week to reading, recognizing and reciprocating true and full history, gaining knowledge of myself, and applying my knowledge of self to improve my social, political and financial position in my country'. We need action. Your 'amen to that', 'tell the truth' and 'preach brother' are all greatly appreciated, but I would much rather have you reading, recognizing and reciprocating, developing knowledge of self, then developing and executing strategies for financial, political and social growth. I would be thrilled to hear of your progress, please email me at nqc@knowledgeofselfpublishing.com.

163

The Solution

European and European Americans, if you really care about creating equality in our country, you must also seek 'What You Were Not Taught'. It may be, no, it will be painful to learn what you were not taught and to insert negative points of your culture into your history, but just know conscious African Americans have been feeling that pain since it has been legal for them to go to school. In order for you to fully respect African and African Americans based on merit and not because the constitution says you should, you must learn the positive aspects of our history. The force taught you that select African Americans, Dr. Martin Luther King, Harriet Tubman, Jesse Jackson, George Washington Carver, Nelson Mandela, Desmond Tutu, should be respected based on their merits. It taught you the balance of African Americans were all slaves who your forefathers whipped, raped, used and abused, but who you should respect because of the Emancipation Proclamation and the 13th, 14th and 15th amendments to the constitution say so. What you were taught would allow you to respect select African and African American individuals based on their merit, but not the aggregate African nor African American culture. For that reason, it is absolutely necessary you learn as many APs as possible.

The men and women of all cultures are equal. Each culture has its ups and its downs, is civilized and uncivilized, is humane and inhumane; we are all equal. Strive to acquire a true and full history of all people to promote equality throughout our country and our planet. Hopefully, the common education and experience you received in the form of this book has enabled you to recognize the other perspective, so you can see each culture in a new light, a light that has exposed the deception of your education. These words I consider the unadulterated truth, the whole truth and nothing but the truth, so help me God. Thank you for reading. You can reach me at my email or www.myspace.com/nquamerecincere.

Endnotes

Foreword

[1] See Dr. Thomas Savage and Professor Jeffries Wyman, "Notice of the External Characters and Habits of Troglodytes Gorilla," *Boston Journal of Natural History* (1847).

[2] See Paul B. Barringer, *The American Negro: His Past and Future* (Raleigh: Edwards & Broughton, 1900).

[3] See Nathaniel Southgate Shaler, "The Negro Problem," Atlantic Monthly 54 (1884) and Nathaniel Southgate Shaler, "Science and the African Problem," The Atlantic Monthly 66 (1890).

[4] See Robert Bennett Bean, *The Races of Man: Differentiation and Dispersal of Man* (New York: University Society, 1935); Robert Bennett Bean, "The Negro Brain," Century Illustrated LXXII (1906); and Robert Bennett Bean, "Some Racial Peculiarities of the Negro Brain," *American Journal of Anatomy* (1906).

[5] See James Henry Breasted, *Ancient Times: A History of the Early World* (Boston: Ginn and Company, 1944).

[6] Direct quotes of many of the individuals listed can be found in Indus Khamit-Kush, *What They Never Told You In History Class* (New York: A&B Publishers Group, 1999). Interested readers can also reference Winthrop D. Jordan, *White Over Black: American Attitudes Toward the Negro 1550-1812* (North Carolina: The University of North Carolina Press, 1968).

Part A: Introduction

[1] Booker T. Washington, *Up From Slavery: An Autobiography* (New York: A.L. Burt Company, 1901), 36.

Knowledge of Self

[1] Washington, 36.

[2] Other Americans such as Mexican Americans, Puerto Rican
Americans, Guamanian Americans, etc. also operate at a
handicap as the education system does not teach them their
ancestry either, but they are not handicapped to the same extent
as African Americans. While the ancestry of other non-European
Americans is more or less ignored, the ancestry of African
Americans is consistently portrayed as occupying the bottom of
the civilization barrel. Nonetheless, they are still subjected to the
portrayal of European Americans as masters of the universe and
the saviors of man-kind and while I feel greatly for these fellow
non-European Americans, I am compelled to write from the
African American perspective since I myself am African
American.

The Force

[1] In reference to the great African General Hannibal Barca's
siege on Rome and the thousands of African troops he left in
Italy after battling the Romans on their home turf. Additionally,
before Hannibal, his father General Hamalcair Barca, African
Pharaoh Senurest I of Egypt and African General Ganges of
Ethiopia also had conquers in Europe and India where naturally
their soldiers procreated with the women to deepen the dark tint
of those peoples skin as well. See Dr. Yosef A. A. ben-
Jochannan, *Black Man of the Nile and His Family* (Baltimore:
Black Classic Press, 1989), 300 and 326.

[2] When I speak of world history throughout this book, it refers to
the teaching of world history in our country, the United States of
America.

Part B: Perspective & History

[1] Cheikh Anta Diop, *The African Origin of Civilization: Myth or
Reality,* edited and translated by Mercer Cook, (Chicago:

166

Perspective

[1] http://www.merriam-webster.com.

[2] http://www.hyperdictionary.com.

The Dominant Perspective

[1] Even as a child, I could never figure out what a 55 year old white woman from the suburbs could counsel an inner city young black male about? Maybe how to bake a cake or create a scrapbook? I wish she could have counseled me how to earn street credibility and keep the killers off my back without having to maim my own people. I believe the janitors (who all happened to be African American men and women from my neighborhood) were more equipped to counsel myself and all my peers than the 55 year old white female counselor.

[2] www.census.gov/popest/national/arch/NC-EST2003-srh.html.

[3] George Washington, *The Writings of George Washington from the Original Manuscript Sources, Volume 2, 1757-1769,* edited by John C. Fitzpatrick, (Washington D.C.: United States Government Printing Office, 1931) 438. I would even go so far to argue that no such person as a black American existed during those times. There were Negroes in America but no Negro Americans. I find it illogical to believe that a man would fight for the freedom of his brother from a common imperialist then turn around and devalue the worth of his brother by only recognizing him as 3/5ths of a person.

[4] As depicted in Figure 4, there will be a few European Americans who do not agree with the interpretation and explanation, but certainly the majority will.

[5] Again, as depicted in Figure 4, there will be a few African Americans who do not agree with the interpretation and explanation, but certainly the majority will.

[6] In fact, *The Negro Almanac: A Reference Work on the African American* notes that "There are 18 slaves in Mount Vernon, Virginia at the time George Washington acquires the estate there. Under Washington, the number grows to 200. Washington's record shows a concern for their physical welfare, but vacillation about their right to freedom and his willingness to dispose with their services. Harry A. Ploski and James Williams comps. and eds., *The Negro Almanac: A Reference Work On The African American,* 5th ed. (Detroit: Gale Research, 1989), 5-7.

[7] Just to throw another angle of perspective on this argument, consider how native English would view George Washington. Since Washington was a proverbial son of England who migrated to America, do you think the people of Great Britain would view Washington a traitor? It seems logical that the British would interpret and explain Washington as an unappreciative ingrate, traitor and conspirator who bit the hand that fed him and murdered his own brethren.

What You Were & Were Not Taught

[1] See Yosef A. A. ben-Jochannan, *Black Man of the Nile and His Family* (Baltimore: Black Classic Press, 1989) 263.

Part C: World History, Perspective & Balance

[1] Dr. John Henrik Clarke, *Who Betrayed The African World Revolution? And Other Speeches* (Chicago: Third World Press, 1994) 88.

Unbalanced Nature of World History

[1] See ben-Jochannan, 160.

[2] John G. Jackson, *Introduction to African Civilizations* (New York: Kensington Publishing Corporation, 1994) 97.

[3] http://www.mnsu.edu/emuseum/prehistory/egypt/history/periods /predynastic.html.

[4] Diop, 251-2.

[5] Jackson, 76.

[6] This is not the last time ancient Europeans will borrow culture from ancient Africans. Later in antiquity, after highly civilized Greeks and Romans had conquered Egypt, the Greeks and Romans stole Egyptian knowledge and adopted many Egyptian religious, medical and cultural practices. See Dr. George G. M. James' *Stolen Legacy* as documented source for stolen knowledge and Zahi Hawass' *Valley of the Golden Mummies* for adopted Egyptian religious beliefs.
George G. M. James, *Stolen Legacy* (Trenton: Africa World Press, 1992). Zahi Hawas, *Valley of the Golden Mummies* (New York: Harry N. Abrams, Incorporated, 2000) 64-7, 121 and 139.

[7] ben-Jochannan, 116. Consistent with the discipline of history, dates very slightly.

What You Were Taught (Dominant Perspective)

[1] I can also recall the Alexander the Grape candy available in any corner store in my neighborhood for 10¢, including the cartoon character on the front of the box wearing a Greek style helmet.

[2] Even as a child, I could never figure out what a 55 year old white woman from the suburbs could counsel an inner city young black male about? Maybe how to bake a cake or create a scrapbook? I wish she could have counseled me how to earn street credibility and keep the killers off my back without having

169

to maim my own people. I believe the janitors (who all happened to be African American men and women from my neighborhood) were more equipped to counsel myself and all my peers than the 55 year old white female counselor.

[3] See ben-Jochannan, 263.

[4] Herodotus translated by Henry Cary, *Herodotus* (425 B.C.?; reprint, New York: Harper & Brothers, 1872) 124.

[5] See ben-Jochannan, 330 and James', *Stolen Legacy*.

[6] Herodotus questions whether Homer wrote another poem as it is believed that the Greek who is given so much credit in our high school and college curriculum stole Egyptian writings and simply put his name on them as if he actually wrote them. Herodotus, 247.

[7] The *Book of Coming Forth To Day From Night* is often times erroneously referred to as the *Egyptian Book of the Dead* to place a negative connotation on an African masterpiece.

[8] See Jackson, 232-263. (See the entire Chapter 6.)

[9] See ben-Jochannan, 257.

[10] Ivan Van Sertima, *They Came Before Columbus: The African Presence In Ancient America* (New York: Random House, 1976).

[11] In his book *What They Never Told You In History Class*, Indus Khamit-Kush writes: "The Ancient Greek Geographer, Strabo, says this about the Ancient Black Egyptian Priests of the City of Thebes:

'The Priests at Thebes are reputed to be the most learned in astronomy and philosophy.'

(Strabo – Bk. XVII, Chap, 1 – Par. 22 – 816)."

Indus Khamit-Kush, *What They Never Told You In History Class* (New York: A&B Publishers Group, 1999) 204-5.

What You Were Not Taught (The Truth)

1 Scynthia is located in northeastern Europe. Ever heard of them? They are some of the most barbaric Europeans that ever lived. Ever wonder why you haven't heard of them?

2 Herodotus, 48-55.

3 Ibid, 183.

4 Ibid, 183-4.

5 Ibid, 61.

6 Ibid, 246.

7 Ibid, 93.

8 Ibid, 42, 86, 93.

9 Ibid, 257-8.

10 *World Timeline: Roman Empire*. History Channel International, 2004.

11 *In Search of History: The Roman Emperors*. A&E Television Networks, 1997. DVD.

12 Dean Dudley, *History of the First Council of Nice: A World's Christian Convention A.D. 325 With A Life of Constantine* (New York: A&B Publishers, 1992) 22.

13 Herodotus, 217-8.

14 Ibid, 100

15 Diop, 49.

16 Khamit-Kush, 147-8. Auguste Mariette, translated by Mary Brodrick, *Outlines of Ancient Egyptian History* (New York: Charles Scribner and Sons, 1892), 10-11.

17 Herodotus, 100.

18 Jackson, 97.

19 George G. M. James, *Stolen Legacy* (Trenton: Africa World Press, 1992) 47.

20 Khamit-Kush, 187. Albert Slosman, *The Book of the Life Beyond* (Paris: Boudouin, 1919).

[21] Ibid, 157. S.R.K. Granville ed., *The Legacy of Egypt* (London: Oxford University Press, 1942), 64-5.

[22] Ibid, 189. Diodorus Siculus, translated by Edwin Murphy, *Diodorus on Egypt,* (Jefferson: McFarland and Company, Inc., 1985).

[23] Herodotus, 224.

[24] ben-Jochannan, 256.

[25] Herodotus, 118-9.

[26] Ibid, 95.

[27] Jackson, 217.

[28] See ben-Jochannan, 44 and 268.

[29] Ibid, 326.

[30] J. A. Rogers, *World's Great Men of Color*, Volume 1 (New York: Touchstone, 1996) 286-294.

Why?

[1] Reference Figure 4. Some anomalies will occur and some Europeans will identify the negative (ex. Herodotus), but the vast majority will not.

Receptiveness to True & Full History

[1] In this instance, a person's intelligence is not defined by or directly linked to their level of formal education. For example, a person with a Below Average Education (B.A.E.) can very well have a high level of intelligence and a person with an Above Average Education (A.A.E.) can be of very low intelligence.

[2] To qualify this statement, significant accomplishments are things such as developing civilization, introducing the concept of farming, mining, etc. to man kind. There are other great accomplishments by other cultures that European Americans openly accept, but I am speaking of significant accomplishments that his third eye will not accept.

The Solution

[1] Actually this supplemental education is extremely important for all non-European Americans such as Jamaican Americans, Mexican Americans, Chinese Americans, Japanese Americans, Guamanian Americans, Native Americans, etc. But since I myself am African American, I write from the African American perspective.

Selected Bibliography

Barashango, Ishakamusa. *Afrikan People and European Holidays: A Mental Genocide, Book One.* Washington D.C.: IVth Dynasty Publishing, Company, 2001.

———. Afrikan People and European Holidays: A Mental Genocide, Book Two. Washington D.C.: IVth Dynasty Publishing, Company, 2001.

ben-Jochannan, Dr. Yosef A. A. Black Man of the Nile and His Family. Baltimore: Black Classic Press, 1989.

Breasted, James Henry. Ancient Times: A History of the Early World. Boston: Ginn and Company, 1944.

Budge, E.A. Wallis. Book of Coming Forth To Day From Night. New York: G.P. Putnam's Sons, 1894.

Clarke, Dr. John Henrik. Who Betrayed The African World Revolution? And Other Speeches. Chicago: Third World Press, 1994.

Delany, Martin R. The Origin of Races And Color. Philadelphia: Harper & Brother Publishers, 1879. Reprint, Baltimore: Black Classic Press, 1991.

Diop, Cheikh Anta. The African Origin of Civilization: Myth or Reality. Edited and translated by Mercer Cook. Chicago: Lawrence Hill Books, 1974.

Dudley, Dean. History of the First Council of Nice: A World's Christian Convention A.D. 325 With A Life of Constantine. New York: A&B Publishers Group, 1992.

Hawas, Zahi. Valley of the Golden Mummies. New York: Harry N. Abrams Incorporated, 2000.

Herodotus. Herodotus. Translated by Henry Cary. New York: Harper & Brothers, 1872.

Jackson, John G. Introduction to African Civilizations. New York: Kensington Publishing Corporation, 1994.

James, George G. M. Stolen Legacy. Trenton: Africa World Press, 1992.

Jordan, Winthrop D. White Over Black: American Attitudes Toward the Negro 1550-1812. North Carolina: The University of North Carolina Press, 1968.

Khamit-Kush, Indus. What They Never Told You In History Class. New York: A&B Publishers Group, 1999.

Ploski, Harry A. and James Williams comps. and eds. The Negro Almanac: A Reference Work On The African American, 5th ed. Detroit: Gale Research, 1989.

Selected Bibliography

Rogers, J. A. World's Great Men of Color, Volume I. New York: Touchstone, 1996.
———. World's Great Men of Color, Volume II. New York: Touchstone, 1996.
———. 100 Amazing Facts About The Negro With Complete Proof: A Short Cut to The World History of The Negro. Florida: Helga M. Rogers, 1995.
Salley, Columbus. The Black 100: A Ranking of the Most Influential African-Americans, Past and Present. New Jersey: Carol Publishing Group, 1999.
Sertima, Ivan Van. They Came Before Columbus: The African Presence In Ancient America. New York: Random House, 1976.
Washington, Booker T. Up From Slavery: An Autobiography. New York: A.L. Burt Company, 1901.
Washington, George. The Writings of George Washington from the Original Manuscript Sources, Volume 2, 1757-1769. Edited by John C. Fitzpatrick. Washington D.C.: United States Government Printing Office, 1931.

Index

Ahmose I *105, 110*
Akhenaten *107, 110*
Alexander *40, 61, 109, 110, 112*
Ali, Sunni *114*
Amenemhet I *103, 109*
Amenemhet III *104, 109*
Amenhotep III *106, 110*
Amenhotep IV *See Akhenaten*
Ancestry *2-6, 142, 162,*
Aphrodite *80*
Ashanti *114*
Astyages, King *75-77*
Babylonian *79, 80*
Barbaric, Barbarism *10, 41, 42, 53, 54, 55, 71, 72, 74, 75, 76, 77, 78, 79, 81, 82, 83, 84, 85, 89, 105, 127, 151*
Barca, Hannibal *114*
ben-Jochannan, Yosef *50, 55, 158*
Bent Pyramid *95*
Berlin Conference *40, 63*
Blood *xvi, 79, 80, 81, 128, 140, 141, 142, 156, 163,*
Boise, Zinjanthropus *88, 104*
Book of Coming Forth To Day From Night *70,*
Caesar, Julius *40, 55, 61, 81, 109, 110*
Caligula *81, 82*
Cambyses *31, 75, 76, 77, 109, 110, 132*
Cannibalism *xix, 74, 75, 122, 127, 140, 141*
Carter, Howard *107*
Cetewayo *43, 114, 115*

Civilization
African *50, 51, 54, 55, 56, 74*
European *54, 55, 56, 57, 60, 61, 62, 63, 74, 127*
Fathers of *6, 42, 43, 89*
Clarke, John Henrik *45, 158*
Claudius *82*
Columbus, Christopher *xiii, 40, 49, 70, 97, 98*
Constantine *40, 61, 83, 84, 141*
Crete *51, 52, 53, 54*
Crispus *83*
Currency *116*
Cyrus *61, 76, 77*
Dahmer, Jeffrey *141*
Delany, Martin R. *37, 158*
Diop, Cheikh Anta *15, 51, 89, 158*
Djoser *93, 94, 95, 109*
Equality *5, 6, 14, 43, 44, 138, 139, 143, 148, 156, 162, 163, 164*
Etymology *29*
Father of History *69, 75, 77, 88, 111*
Forten, James *37*
Ganges, General *114*
Garnett, Henry Highland *36, 158*
Garvey, Marcus *36, 37, 158*
Gein, Ed *141*
Gelasius, Pope *113*
Gibral, Tarikh *114*
Giza *96, 97, 99, 101*
Great Pyramid *93, 96, 97, 99*

Index

Index

Special thanks to:

Afrikan World Books

2217 Pennsylvania Avenue
Baltimore, MD 21217

Phone: 410-383-2006
Fax: 410-383-0511

Email: sales@afrikanworldbooks.com
Web: www.afrikanworldbooks.com

Knowledge of Self Publishing, LLC
ORDER FORM

Who in your life can benefit from the knowledge in this book? You must know someone who will find it enlightening, interesting, inspirational or empowering. ***Why not order them a copy?***

Internet Orders: www.knowledgeofselfpublishing.com
Email Orders: order@knowledgeofselfpublishing.com
Fax Orders: Fax this page to 301-994-9039.
Telephone Orders: Call 240-298-4165.
Mail Orders: Fill out the below form and mail it to
Knowledge of Self Publishing, LLC
P.O. Box 1010
California, Maryland 20619

Name:					
Address:					
City:		State:		Zip:	
Phone:		Email:			

Product	Qty	X	Price	=	Total
We Ain't		X	$18.00	=	
No Niggas!	Tax	State of Maryland residents please add 5%		=	
Exposing the Deception of YOUR World	Shipping (U.S.P.S. Priority Mail)	$4.50 for first book and $2.00 each addtl. book		=	
History Education	Total			=	

Payment: ☐Check*   Credit Card: ☐ Visa   ☐MasterCard
☐ Discover   ☐ AMEX

Cardholder's Name:	
Card Number:	
Expiration Date:	

*Make checks payable to: **Knowledge of Self Publishing, LLC**

THANK YOU FOR YOUR BUSINESS!
100% Money Back Guarantee!